366
RECIPES

QUICK
AND
EASY

SUNBURST BOOKS

This edition first published in 1994 by
Sunburst Books, Deacon House, 65 Old Church Street,
London, SW3 5BS.

Copyright © 1994 Sunburst Books

ISBN 1 85778 058 2

Printed and bound in India

CONTENTS

Soups *6*

Snacks and Sandwiches *12*

Beef *26*

Pork *39*

Lamb *54*

Offal *65*

Poultry *75*

Fish *88*

Cheese and Eggs *103*

Rice and Pasta *118*

Vegetables *136*

Salads *143*

Desserts *153*

Cakes and Biscuits *172*

Index *189*

SOUPS

KIDNEY AND ONION SOUP
Serves 6

8 oz (225 g) ox kidney
1 oz (25 g) suet
1 large onion, chopped
2 pt (1.1 ltr) beef stock
2 tsp tomato puree
1 bay leaf
good pinch of mixed herbs
salt and pepper
1 tbsp cornflour
2 tbsp sherry

Decore the kidney and chop into small pieces. Melt the suet in a saucepan, add the kidney and onion and cook for 5 minutes, stirring from time to time. Pour in the stock, tomato puree, bay leaf and herbs, and add salt and pepper to taste. Bring to the boil, lower heat, cover and simmer for 20 minutes until the kidney is tender. Remove the bay leaf. Place the sherry and cornflour in a blender and blend well. Add some of the soup and puree. Transfer to a bowl. Puree the remaining soup and pour into the bowl. Return all the soup to the saucepan and bring to the boil, stirring. Add more salt and pepper if required. Pour into bowls and serve immediately.

APPLE AND CASHEW SOUP
Serves 4

1 onion
4 oz (110 g) button mushrooms
4 oz (110 g) cashew nuts
1 pt (600 ml) apple juice
salt and pepper
1/2 tsp dried mixed herbs
1 tsp yeast extract

Chop the onion and slice the mushrooms in half. Place these together with all the other ingredients in a large saucepan. Bring to the boil, lower heat and simmer for 10 minutes. Pour the soup into individual soup bowls and serve accompanied by warm French bread.

CHICKEN AND SWEETCORN CHOWDER
Serves 4

1 tbsp sunflower oil
1 onion, chopped
1 garlic clove, chopped
2 medium potatoes, diced
1 pt (600 ml) chicken stock
1 bay leaf
salt and pepper
1 x 11 oz (325 g) can of sweetcorn, drained
6 oz (175 g) cooked chicken, chopped
2 tbsp chopped fresh parsley

Heat the oil in a pan and fry the onion and garlic until soft. Stir in the potatoes, chicken stock and bay leaf, and add salt and pepper to taste. Cook for 15 minutes over medium heat. Add the sweetcorn, chicken and parsley and simmer over low heat for 5 minutes. Serve immediately accompanied by crusty bread.

WHITE FISH CHOWDER
Serves 6

2 rashers rindless bacon
1 lb (450 g) white fish, such as coley, haddock or cod
2 oz (50 g) butter
4 medium-sized potatoes, peeled and diced
2 leeks, sliced into rings
2 oz (50 g) button mushrooms
1 pt (600 ml) milk
salt and pepper
pinch of grated nutmeg
1 x 8 oz (225 g) can of tomatoes

Dice the bacon and place in a frying pan. Cook in its own fat until crisp. Chop the fish into small pieces and discard the skin and bones. Place the butter in a saucepan over low heat and, when melted, add the fish, potatoes, leeks and mushrooms. Cook for 2 minutes, then gradually stir in the milk and simmer gently for 15-20 minutes. Add nutmeg and salt and pepper to taste. Gently stir in the bacon and tomatoes and heat through. Pour into individual soup bowls and serve immediately.

MUSHROOM AND SHERRY SOUP
Serves 6

1 lb (450 g) button mushrooms
1 onion, chopped
2 garlic cloves, crushed
2 oz (50 g) butter
2 oz (50 g) plain flour
½ pt (300 ml) milk
1 pt (600 ml) chicken stock
2 tbsp sherry
salt and pepper
single cream and chopped parsley, to garnish

Melt the butter in a saucepan, add the onion and garlic and cook until soft. Thinly slice the mushrooms and add to the onion. Cook gently for a few minutes. Gradually stir in the flour and blend in the milk and stock. Bring to the boil, reduce the heat and simmer for 15 minutes, stirring frequently. Pour in the sherry and add salt and pepper to taste. Pour into individual soup bowls, adding a swirl of cream on top with a sprinkling of parsley. Serve immediately.

CARROT AND CELERY SOUP
Serves 6

1½ lb (675 g) carrots, sliced
1 onion
2 celery sticks
1 oz (25 g) butter
1 oz (25 g) plain flour
1½ pt (900 ml) chicken stock
1 x 14 oz (400 g) can evaporated milk
2 tsp lemon juice
grated carrots and chopped parsley, to garnish

Place the carrots in boiling, salted water and cook for 15 minutes. Drain well. Melt the butter in a frying pan, chop the onion and celery and cook in the melted butter until softened. Lower the heat and stir in the flour. Add the carrots and gradually pour in the milk and stock, stirring constantly. Pour in the lemon juice. Bring to the boil, lower heat and simmer for 5 minutes. Add salt and pepper to taste. Transfer the soup to a liquidiser and blend thoroughly. Return to the saucepan and heat through. Pour into individual soup bowls and garnish with the carrot and parsley.

FRENCH ONION SOUP
Serves 6

1 lb (450 g) onions
2 oz (50 g) butter
1³/₄ pt (1 ltr) beef stock
¹/₄ pt (150 ml) dry red wine
salt and pepper
6 slices of French bread, buttered
4 oz (110 g) Gruyère cheese, grated

Chop the onions. Melt the butter in a frying pan, add the onions and cook until soft and golden. Add the stock, bring to the boil, lower heat and simmer for 25 minutes. Pour in the wine and add salt and pepper to taste. Stir well and cook for a few minutes. Place a slice of French bread into each of 6 heatproof soup bowls, then pour over the soup. When the bread has risen to the surface, sprinkle over the Gruyère cheese and cook under a hot grill until the cheese is bubbly and golden brown. Serve at once.

CHEESE AND ONION SOUP
Serves 6

2 onions
2 oz (50 g) butter
2 oz (50 g) plain flour
1 pt (600 ml) chicken stock
1 pt (600 ml) milk
8 oz (225 g) mature Cheddar cheese, grated
¹/₄ pt (150 ml) dry cider
¹/₄ tsp grated nutmeg
salt and pepper
some grated cheese and croutons, to garnish

Melt the butter in a saucepan, chop the onions and cook in the butter for 3-4 minutes until soft. Lower the heat and stir in the flour. Gradually pour in the stock, followed by the milk, stirring constantly. Bring to the boil and cook for 3-4 minutes. Remove from the heat, add the Cheddar cheese and stir well until the cheese has melted. Replace over low heat, pour in the cider and add salt and pepper to taste, stirring well. Do not let the soup boil. Pour into individual soup bowls, garnish with grated cheese and croutons and serve immediately.

CURRIED PARSNIP SOUP
Serves 6

1 onion
2 garlic cloves
1½ lb (675 g) parsnips, peeled
1 tart dessert apple, peeled and cored
2 tbsp oil
1 tbsp curry powder
1½ oz (35 g) flour
2 pt (1.1 ltr) chicken stock
salt and pepper
natural yoghurt, to garnish

Chop the onion, garlic, parsnips and apple. Pour the oil into a saucepan and, when heated, add the curry powder, vegetables and apple and cook for 5 minutes. Lower the heat and gradually stir in the flour. Pour in the stock, stirring constantly. Bring to the boil, add salt and pepper to taste, lower the heat and simmer for 20 minutes. Transfer the soup to a liquidiser and blend well until smooth. Return the soup to the saucepan and heat through. Pour into individual soup bowls and garnish with a swirl of yoghurt.

CREAM OF WATERCRESS SOUP
Serves 6

1 onion, chopped
2 garlic cloves, crushed
2 oz (50 g) butter
2 oz (50 g) plain flour
1 pt (600 ml) chicken stock
1 pt (600 ml) milk
2 bunches of watercress, trimmed and chopped
salt and pepper
½ tsp grated nutmeg
juice of half a lemon
¼ pt (150 ml) single cream

Melt the butter in a saucepan, add the onion and garlic and cook until soft. Lower the heat, stir in the flour and gradually pour in the stock and milk, stirring constantly. Stir in the watercress, salt and pepper to taste, nutmeg and lemon juice. Simmer over low heat for 5 minutes. Remove from the heat and stir in the cream. Gently reheat and pour the soup into individual bowls. Serve at once.

DUTCH PEPPER SOUP
Serves 4

2 tbsp vegetable oil
2 oz (50 g) butter
8 oz (225 g) red or green peppers, deseeded and diced
2 onions, chopped
1½ oz (35 g) flour
¾ pt (450 ml) chicken stock
salt and pepper
¾ pt (450 ml) milk
2-3 tbsp single cream

Heat the oil and butter in a saucepan. Add the peppers and onions
and cook for 5 minutes, stirring occasionally. Gradually stir in the
flour and cook for 1 minute. Pour in the stock and bring to the boil,
stirring until the soup has thickened. Add salt and pepper to taste,
cover and simmer over low heat for 30 minutes until the vegetables
are soft. Transfer to the liquidiser and blend well. Return to the
saucepan and pour in the milk. Bring to the boil, add more salt and
pepper, if required, then stir in the cream. Pour into individual bowls
and serve at once.

CREAM OF SPINACH SOUP
Serves 4

2 oz (50 g) butter
2 onions, chopped
2 oz (50 g) flour
1½ pt (900 ml) chicken stock
1 x 10 oz (300 g) packet of frozen spinach
pinch of nutmeg
salt and pepper
¼ pt (150 ml) single cream

Melt the butter in a saucepan and add the onion. Cook for 10 minutes
until the onion is soft. Stir in the flour and cook for 1 minute. Pour in
the stock and bring to the boil, stirring until thickened. Add the block
of spinach followed by the nutmeg and salt and pepper to taste. Cover
and simmer for 15 minutes until the spinach is cooked. Transfer the
soup to a liquidiser and blend well. Return the soup to the saucepan
and heat through, adding more salt and pepper if required. Stir in the
cream and serve at once.

VEGETABLE SOUP
Serves 6

1 lb (450 g) old potatoes
1 lb (450 g) carrots
2 leeks, sliced
2 oz (50 g) butter
2 pt (1.1 ltr) chicken stock
salt and pepper
¼ pt (150 ml) milk

Grate the potatoes and carrots and mix them with the leeks. Place the butter in a saucepan over low heat and, when melted, add the vegetables. Cover and cook for about 10 minutes. Pour in the stock with salt and pepper to taste. Cover the saucepan and simmer for 30 minutes until the vegetables are tender. Pour in the milk, stirring well, and serve at once.

SNACKS & SANDWICHES

CROQUE MONSIEUR
Serves 1

2 thin slices of white bread
½ oz (10 g) softened butter
2 thin slices Gruyère cheese
1 slice cooked ham, cut to the same size as the bread
oil for frying

Spread butter on one slice of bread. Cover with one slice of cheese, the slice of ham, and then the second slice of cheese. Butter the second slice of bread and press it face down on top of the cheese. Trim off the crusts. Heat the remaining butter together with a little oil in a frying pan. Put the sandwich in the pan and cook for about 3 minutes on each side until the cheese has melted and the bread has browned.

SANDWICH KEBABS
Serves 4

4 slices streaky bacon, rinds removed
12 cocktail frankfurters
6 slices soft-grain sliced bread
margarine for spreading
4 oz (110 g) Cheddar cheese, sliced
4 oz (110 g) Red Leicester cheese, sliced
3 in (7.5 cm) piece of cucumber
2 sticks celery, wiped and cut into 1 in (2.5 cm) pieces
6 oz (175 g) can pineapple cubes, drained

Cut each slice of bacon into three and wrap each piece around a frankfurter. Secure with cocktail sticks and grill for 4-5 minutes, turning frequently until golden brown. Set aside. Spread the bread with the margarine and place a slice of Cheddar cheese on two slices, place another slice of bread on top and then put the Red Leicester on these, topping with the remaining two slices of bread. Press down firmly, trim the crusts and cut each layered sandwich into four. Cut the cucumber into four thin slices. If the cucumber is a large one, cut the pieces in half. Using wooden kebab skewers, push the various items alternately onto the skewer using three bacon rolls, two mini sandwiches and one piece each of the cucumber, celery and pineapple for each skewer.

SMOKED CHICKEN AND CHEESE TOASTS
Serves 4

8 slices coarse-grain rye bread
4 oz (110 g) smoked chicken, sliced
6 oz (175 g) goat's cheese, thinly sliced

Place the bread under the grill and toast on one side only. Place a slice of chicken on top of the untoasted side of bread, followed by a slice of cheese. Cook under the grill until the cheese is beginning to brown. Serve immediately.

HAM AND CREAM CHEESE TRIPLE-DECKER
Makes 4

8 slices brown bread
8 slices white bread, buttered
4 oz (110 g) cream cheese
1 small onion, very finely chopped
4 oz (110 g) ham, minced
1 tbsp mayonnaise
a dash of Worcestershire sauce
2 tomatoes, sliced
salt
chopped basil

Beat the cream cheese and very finely chopped onion together and spread on one slice of brown bread. Cover with another slice of brown bread. Mix the minced ham, Worcestershire sauce and mayonnaise together. Spread this on top of the brown sandwich and cover with a buttered slice of white bread. Cover this with sliced tomatoes, a sprinkling of salt and chopped basil and top with a further slice of white bread. Cut into quarters to serve.

CHICKEN LIVER BAGELS
Serves 4

2 tbsp oil
1 onion, chopped
2 garlic cloves, chopped
8 oz (225 g) chicken livers
1 tbsp chopped fresh parsley
1 tsp chopped fresh thyme
salt and pepper
2 bagels
1 oz (25 g) butter
4 cherry tomatoes

Pour the oil into a pan and heat. Add the onion and cook over low heat until soft. Stir in the garlic and chicken livers and cook for 5 minutes until the livers are slightly pink inside. Add the parsley and thyme with salt and pepper to taste and cook for a further 2 minutes. Remove the livers, chop them roughly and return them to the pan to warm through. Cut the bagels in half and toast the cut sides. Spread over the butter and place a tomato in the middle of each half. Arrange the liver mixture on and around the top and serve immediately.

MUFFIN PIZZAS
Serves 4

4 tbsp tomato puree
2 tbsp olive oil
1 tbsp chopped fresh basil (or 1½ tsp dried)
freshly ground black pepper
4 wholemeal muffins
2 beef tomatoes
4 oz (110 g) salami, cubed
6 oz (175 g) Mozzarella cheese, cubed
2 yellow peppers, seeded and diced

Cut each of the muffins in half. Mix together the tomato puree, 1 tbsp of the oil and half of the fresh or dried basil. Season with pepper. Spread over the muffin halves. Slice the tomatoes and place one slice on top of each muffin. Add the cubes of salami and yellow peppers, and top with the Mozzarella cheese. Sprinkle with the remaining basil and drizzle a little olive oil over the top. Place under a hot grill for 4-5 minutes or until the cheese has melted and browned. Serve with a crisp salad.

CHICKEN LIVERS ON TOAST
Serves 4

4 oz (110 g) chicken livers
seasoned flour
butter for frying
4 rounds of bread, about 2 in (5 cm) in diameter
½ glass sherry
2 oz (50 g) mushrooms, wiped and sliced

Wash and dry the chicken livers. Cut into small pieces and dust thoroughly with the seasoned flour. Melt the butter in a small frying pan and fry the bread for 2 minutes on each side until golden. Remove from the pan and keep warm. Add more butter and sauté the sliced mushrooms for about 5 minutes until cooked through. Remove from the pan and keep warm. Wipe out the pan, add more butter and gently fry the chicken livers, turning them over, until browned. Pour in the sherry, mix well and cook slowly for another 10 minutes. Spoon a mixture of mushrooms and livers onto each slice of fried bread and serve hot.

CREAMED HAM ON TOAST

cooked ham and/or chicken
thick white sauce
thick white bread

Finely chop or process the ham and/or chicken and mix with a thick white sauce, well seasoned. Toast the bread on one side only and spread the untoasted side thickly with the ham mix. Put under the grill for a few minutes.

SPICY HAM AND CHEESE TOASTS

slices of cooked ham
sweet chutney
slices of Cheddar or Gruyère cheese
slices of thick white bread

Toast the bread and butter it liberally. Put a slice of ham on each piece of toast, spread with chutney and cover with a slice of cheese. Put under a hot grill until the cheese melts.

CORNED BEEF AND SWEETCORN DOUBLE-DECKER
Serves 1

2 slices white bread, buttered
1 slice brown bread, buttered
2 oz (50 g) corned beef, sliced
1 oz (25 g) canned sweetcorn, drained
1 tsp mayonnaise
mustard
salt and pepper

Lay the corned beef over one slice of white bread and spread with a little mustard (or sweet pickle if preferred). Cover with the brown slice, buttered side down. Mix together the sweetcorn and mayonnaise and season to taste. Spread over the brown slice and press down the remaining white slice, buttered side down. Cut in half diagonally and serve with tomato wedges.

HAM AND CHICKEN DOUBLE-DECKER
Serves 1

2 slices wholemeal bread
1 slice white bread
1 oz (25 g) smoked ham
1 spring onion, trimmed and cut diagonally
few sprigs watercress
mustard
butter
2 lettuce leaves, washed and dried
2 oz (50 g) cooked skinned chicken, sliced or shredded
lemon mayonnaise
1 tsp chopped fresh chives
1 tomato, skinned and deseeded, then chopped

Spread one slice of the brown bread with mixed mustard and butter and top with the ham, watercress and spring onion. Spread the white slice with butter and put on top of the ham mixture. Mix the shredded chicken with the lemon mayonnaise, chopped chives and chopped tomato. Season to taste. Place on top of the white bread and press the remaining brown slice on top. Place on a plate, cut in half with a sharp knife and decorate with the two crisp lettuce leaves.

CHICKEN AND MUSHROOM SANDWICHES
Serves 2

4 slices soft-grain white bread
a little butter
4 oz (110 g) sliced cooked chicken
1/2 bunch watercress, washed and trimmed
2 oz (50 g) mushrooms, wiped and sliced
1/2 small can sweetcorn, drained
Greek yoghurt
salt and freshly ground black pepper

Lightly butter the bread on one side only. Place the chicken and watercress on two slices. Mix the mushrooms and sweetcorn with the Greek yoghurt and season well. Spoon over the chicken and place the remaining slices on top, pressing down very gently. Cut the sandwiches in half and decorate with a few remaining watercress sprigs.

CHINESE DRUMSTICKS
Serves 4

8 chicken drumsticks
4 tbsp red wine vinegar
2 tbsp tomato paste
2 tbsp soy sauce
2 tbsp clear honey
1 tbsp Worcestershire sauce
2 cloves garlic, crushed
good pinch of cayenne pepper
salt and pepper

Cut a couple of slashes in the fleshy part of each drumstick and lay them in a shallow dish. Mix all the remaining ingredients together and pour over the chicken. If possible leave in the refrigerator overnight, but if this is not possible, marinade the drumsticks for at least 2 hours. Grill the drumsticks for about 20-30 minutes, turning frequently and basting with the marinade. Serve hot or cold with noodles or a crisp green salad.

CHICKEN AND TOMATO SCRAMBLE
Serves 4

1 tbsp olive oil
½ oz (10 g) butter
4 spring onions, thinly sliced
12 oz (350 g) tomatoes, skinned and chopped
salt and pepper
6 eggs
8 oz (225 g) cooked chicken, chopped
2 tbsp fresh basil chopped
toast triangles, to serve

Melt the butter and oil in a frying pan. Fry the onions for 1 minute, stirring constantly. Stir in the tomatoes and salt and pepper to taste and cook for 2 minutes. Place the eggs in a bowl and beat well. Mix in the chicken and basil and pour the mixture into the frying pan. Lightly stir and cook over low heat until egg is cooked. To serve, pile on individual plates accompanied by the toast triangles.

SAVOURY FRITTERS

Fritter batter:
4 oz (110 g) wholewheat or white self-raising flour
½ level tsp salt
freshly ground black pepper
1 large egg
¼ pint (150 ml) milk
oil for frying

Fillings:
Spam: 1 tin cut in slices and dipped in the batter.
Bacon: 8 oz (225 g) streaky bacon, grilled or fried and cut in strips
Cheese: 6 oz (175 g) grated mature Cheddar
Chicken and mushrooms: 4 oz (110 g) finely chopped cooked chicken mixed
with 2 oz (50 g) chopped mushrooms fried in a little butter
Sweetcorn: 7 oz (200 g) can sweetcorn with peppers, drained

Mix the flour, salt and pepper in a bowl, make a well in the centre and break in the egg. Start working the flour into the egg with a wooden spoon, gradually adding the milk. Beat well until smooth. Stir one of the above fillings into the batter and shallow-fry tablespoonfuls of the mixture until the fritters are golden brown on both sides. Serve with a fresh green salad.

INDIAN PITTAS
Serves 4

4 x 4 oz (110 g) boneless chicken breasts
6 tbsp tandoori paste
6 tbsp natural yoghurt
1 tsp lemon juice
2 tbsp olive oil
4 pitta breads
4 tomatoes
4 lettuce leaves, shredded

Skin the chicken breasts and cut in half horizontally. Mix together the tandoori paste, yoghurt and lemon juice and brush over the chicken. Lay the chicken breasts in a grill pan and drizzle over the olive oil. Grill for 15 minutes, turning over half-way through the cooking. Grill the pitta breads until they puff up, then halve and split them. Cut the chicken into thick slices and fill the pitta breads, tucking in some shredded lettuce as well. Chop the tomatoes and serve on the plate next to the pittas.

SMOKED MACKEREL AND EGG
DOUBLE-DECKER
Serves 1

2 slices white bread, buttered
1 slice brown bread, buttered
2 oz (50 g) smoked mackerel fillets, cooked and skinned
1 oz (25 g) softened butter
a little lemon juice
cucumber slices
1 size 3 egg, hard-boiled
1 tsp whipped cream
lettuce leaves
salt and pepper

Remove any bones from the mackerel, break up the flesh and beat it
with the butter and lemon juice to a smooth paste. Season with pepper. Spread over one slice of white bread and arrange the cucumber
slices on top. Cover with a slice of brown bread. Shell the egg, chop it
very finely and mix with the whipped cream and seasoning. Spread
the egg filling on top of the brown slice, cover with lettuce leaves, add
the remaining white slice of bread and press together gently. Cut into
halves.

SCOTCH WOODCOCK
Serves 4

1 slice of bread from a large loaf
butter
2 oz (50 g) can anchovies, drained and steeped in milk
1/2 oz (10 g) butter
2 tbsp top of the milk
1 large egg
salt and pepper
paprika pepper to garnish

Toast the bread, remove the crusts, butter and cut into triangles.
Reserving 2 anchovy fillets for garnish, sieve the rest and spread on
the toast triangles. Whisk together the milk, egg and seasoning and
pour onto the melted butter in a saucepan. Stir over a low heat until
the mixture begins to thicken, then remove from the heat and keep
stirring until the mixture is creamy. Spread on top of the anchovy
toast and garnish with strips of anchovy and a dash of paprika pepper.

CRAB TOASTS
Serves 4

butter
1 oz (25 g) fresh white breadcrumbs
3½ oz (85 g) can crab meat
3 tbsp single cream
salt and pepper
1 tbsp sherry
4 slices toast

Melt 1 oz (25 g) butter in a saucepan, add the breadcrumbs and flaked crab meat, mix well and stir in the single cream. Season to taste. Stir over a gentle heat, then stir in the sherry. Cut the toast into triangles, removing the crusts, butter and pile high with the crab meat mixture.

MUSHROOM MUFFINS
Serves 4

4 large, flat mushrooms
2 tbsp oil
salt and pepper
8 rashers streaky bacon
4 wholemeal muffins, split
5 eggs
4 tbsp creamy milk
2 tsp snipped chives
1½ oz (35 g) butter

Lightly brush the oil over the mushrooms and sprinkle with salt and pepper to taste. Place on a baking sheet, together with the bacon, and cook under a hot grill, turning once, until cooked. Keep warm. Lightly toast the muffins on both sides and keep warm. Place the eggs, milk and chives in a bowl and beat together thoroughly. Melt the butter in a frying pan, add the egg mixture and cook for 3-4 minutes, stirring constantly, until scrambled. Sandwich each muffin together using two bacon rashers, one mushroom and a portion of the egg. Serve immediately.

ANCHOVY TOASTS
Serves 4

2 slices bread
¹/₂ oz (10 g) butter
squeeze of lemon juice
5 anchovy fillets, chopped
pepper
pinch of ground nutmeg
pinch of ground mace
fresh parsley, chopped

Toast the bread and cut into fingers. Melt the butter, add a squeeze of lemon juice, the chopped anchovies, pepper, nutmeg and mace. Beat well and rub through a sieve. Spread onto the toast fingers and garnish with sprigs of parsley. A similar snack may be made using sardines instead of anchovies. Decorate with a twist of lemon.

KIDNEY BEAN RAREBIT
Serves 4

1 oz (25 g) butter
1 medium-sized onion, finely chopped
1 garlic clove, crushed
1 green pepper, deseeded, white pith removed and finely chopped
14 oz (400 g) can of kidney beans
14 oz (400 g) can of baked beans
4 tbsp tomato ketchup
1 tbsp Worcestershire sauce
¹/₂ tsp salt
1 tsp black pepper
2 tsp mild chilli powder
6 oz (175 g) Cheddar cheese, grated
4 large slices hot buttered toast

Melt the butter in a frying pan over medium heat. When the foam subsides, add the onion, garlic and green pepper and fry, stirring occasionally, for 5-7 minutes until the onion is soft but not brown. Stir in the kidney beans, baked beans (including the sauce), ketchup, Worcestershire sauce, salt, pepper and chilli powder. Cook for 5 minutes, stirring occasionally. Add the cheese and cook, stirring constantly, for 3 minutes until the cheese has melted and the mixture is hot and thick. Remove from the heat and spoon out the mixture onto each toast slice. Serve immediately.

WELSH RAREBIT
Serves 4

8 oz (225 g) Gloucester, Cheddar or Lancashire cheese, grated
1 oz (25 g) butter
1 tsp English mustard
½ tsp black pepper
2-3 tbsp ale
4 slices buttered toast

Melt the cheese and butter in a heavy-based saucepan over low heat. Add the mustard, pepper and ale and continue to stir until the mixture is smooth and creamy. Divide the mixture between the slices of toast and cook under the grill until brown and bubbly.

DEVILLED CHEESE
Serves 6

8 oz (225 g) Cheddar cheese, finely grated
4 tsp chutney
3 tsp curry powder
6 slices white bread, toasted, buttered and kept hot

Preheat the grill. Mix together the cheese, chutney and curry powder. Spread the mixture on one side of each slice of toast and place under the grill at moderate heat for 4 minutes or until the mixture is bubbling. Serve at once.

EGG AND CHIVE SANDWICHES
Makes 8

2 hard-boiled eggs, shelled
2 tbsp mayonnaise
2 tsp fresh chives, chopped
2 oz (50 g) butter, softened
2 large thin slices of brown bread, crusts removed
2 large thin slices of white bread, crusts removed

Mash the eggs in a bowl. Add the mayonnaise and chives and season to taste. Mix thoroughly. Butter each slice of brown bread, spread the egg mixture over, butter the slices of white bread and place on top of each slice of brown bread. Cut each sandwich into four to serve.

SOFT ROE FINGERS
Serves 4

12 soft herring roes
butter for frying
2 slices of white bread, crusts removed
squeeze of lemon juice
fresh chopped parsley

Cut each slice of bread in half lengthwise. Wash the roes, dry them well and fry gently in the melted butter for about 10 minutes until golden. Remove from the pan and keep warm. Wipe out the pan thoroughly and fry the bread fingers in more butter for about 2 minutes each side. Place the cooked roes on the fried bread with a squeeze of lemon juice. Season and sprinkle freshly chopped parsley on top.

PITTA POCKETS
Serves 4

4 plain or wholemeal pitta breads
4 tbsp houmus
4 oz (110 g) Feta cheese
8 cherry tomatoes, slices
1/2 small lettuce, washed and shredded
pimiento stuffed green olives
Greek yoghurt

Slice open the pitta bread along the side with a sharp knife, taking care not to cut through the bread itself. Spread the inside of each pitta with the houmus. Mix together the remaining ingredients, apart from the lettuce, using the Greek yoghurt to bind. Season. Put some of the shredded lettuce in the pitta, then spoon in the cheese and yoghurt mixture and tuck in some more lettuce on top.

CHEESE AND APPLE SANDWICHES
Makes 8

1 1/2 oz (35 g) butter, softened
1/2 oz (10 g) walnuts, chopped
4 square slices light rye bread, crusts removed
4 slices of Brie cheese cut 1/4 in (0.5 cm) thick
1/2 green dessert apple
1/2 red dessert apple
1 tbsp lemon juice

Mix the butter and walnuts in a bowl. Spread this mixture over the bread slices. Cut the cheese in half and arrange 2 pieces on each slice of bread. Quarter and core the apples, but do not peel. Slice the apples thinly and dip in the lemon juice. Arrange overlapping slices of apples, alternating green and red, on top of the cheese. Cut each slice of bread in half diagonally and serve.

RED LEICESTER AND SALAD DOUBLE-DECKER
Serves 1

2 slices white bread, buttered
1 slice brown bread, buttered
1 oz (25 g) Red Leicester cheese, grated
1 tsp mayonnaise
pinch of cayenne pepper
1 tomato, sliced
cucumber slices
few lettuce leaves

Mix the grated cheese, mayonnaise and pepper together and spread on a slice of white bread. Add the tomato slices, season and cover with the slice of brown bread. Add a layer of cucumber and lettuce and cover with the remaining slice of white bread. Press together gently and cut in half diagonally.

INDIAN SCRAMBLE
Serves 2

1 small onion, skinned and chopped
butter
1½ level tsp curry powder
4 eggs
1 tsp fresh parsley, chopped
3 tbsp milk
salt and freshly ground pepper
2 large slices buttered toast

Sauté the onion in the butter until soft but not coloured, then add the curry powder and fry slowly for 5 minutes. Beat together the eggs, seasoning, milk and parsley and add to the pan. Cook gently, stirring all the time and lifting the egg from the base of the pan. Serve on hot buttered toast.

BUCK RAREBIT
Serves 4

8 oz (225 g) Cheddar cheese, grated
1 oz (25 g) butter
1 level tsp dry mustard
salt and freshly ground black pepper
3-4 tbsp brown ale
4 eggs
4 large slices bread
butter

Place the cheese, butter, mustard, seasoning and ale in a heavy saucepan and heat very gently until a creamy mixture is obtained. Poach the eggs in gently simmering water and toast the bread. Spread the toast with butter, pour the hot cheese mixture over and pop under the grill until golden and bubbling. Top each slice with a poached egg and serve.

BEEF

BEEF DARIOLES
Serves 6

3 eggs
8 oz (225 g) sweetcorn
¼ pint (150 ml) milk
8 oz (225 g) minced cooked beef
pinch grated nutmeg
3 medium sized tomatoes, skinned, halved and deseeded

Preheat the oven to 180°C/350°F/Gas Mk 4. Grease 6 dariole moulds with butter and put half a tomato in the base of each mould. Beat the eggs well with the milk and stir in the minced beef, sweetcorn and plenty of seasoning. Pour the mixture into the dariole moulds and bake for about 25 minutes in the oven until the custard sets.

ZEUS STEAKS
Serves 4

2 tbsp oil
4 sirloin or rump steaks
1 lamb's kidney, skinned, cored and sliced
1 oz (25 g) butter
1 large onion, sliced
2 tomatoes, skinned, deseeded and chopped
1 green pepper, deseeded and chopped
¼ pint (150 ml) red wine
¼ pint (150 ml) beef stock
pinch of oregano
salt and pepper

Place the kidney, butter, onion, tomatoes and pepper in a saucepan and cook gently for 5 minutes until tender. Add the wine and stock, season with salt and pepper to taste and add oregano. Bring to the boil and then simmer for 5 minutes to thicken. Heat the oil in a frying pan and cook the steaks for 2-8 minutes according to taste. Pour the sauce over the steaks and serve immediately.

STEAK AND ONIONS

8 oz (225 g) rump steak, 1 in (2.5 cm) thick per person
6 oz (175 g) onions per portion
salt and freshly ground black pepper
butter

Trim the excess fat from the steaks and season the meat to taste. Peel and slice the onions. Sauté the onions in a little melted butter, stirring frequently, until they are soft and golden, but not browned. Lift out and drain on kitchen paper. Keep hot. Add the steak to the pan and cook it quickly, turning from side to side until it is evenly browned and tender. Then remove from the pan and place on a serving dish with the onions. Swill out the pan with a little wine or stock, stir well, season and strain over the steak. Or serve with a pat of herb or parsley butter if preferred.

BEEF AND CASHEW STIR-FRY
Serves 4

2 tbsp sesame oil
12 oz (350 g) rump steak, cut into thin strips
2 carrots, peeled and cut into strips
1 red-skinned onion, cut into strips
1 clove garlic, crushed
1 yellow pepper, wiped, deseeded and diced
4 oz (110 g) baby corn, halved
4 oz (110 g) mangetout
4 oz (110 g) button mushrooms, sliced
1 small fennel bulb, finely chopped
4 oz (110 g) cashew nuts
2 spring onions, sliced
small piece grated fresh ginger
2 tsp sweet chilli sauce
1 tbsp soy sauce
salt and freshly ground black pepper

Heat the oil in a wok and fry the steak for 5 minutes. Add the carrots, onion, garlic, pepper, corn, mangetout, mushrooms and fennel. Stir-fry for 10 minutes, then add the nuts, spring onions, ginger and sauces. Fry for a further 5 minutes. Serve at once with fluffy white rice.

CURRIED MINCE WITH APRICOTS
Serves 4

12 oz (350 g) long-grain rice
1¹/₂ pints (900 ml) chicken stock
4 oz (110 g) dried apricots, halved
1 lb (450 g) minced beef
2 onions, peeled and chopped
1-2 tbsp curry powder

Put the rice, stock and apricots in a large pan and simmer for about 20 minutes until the rice is tender and most of the stock has been absorbed. Fry the meat and onion in a non-stick frying pan for about 5 minutes. Add the curry powder, then continue cooking until golden. Toss the meat mixture into the rice and stock mixture and serve immediately with poppadums and a side salad.

GIANT SPICY BEEFBURGERS
Serves 4

8 oz (225 g) onions, peeled and sliced thinly
1 lb (450 g) minced beef
5 fl oz (150 ml) natural yoghurt
2 level tbsp cornflour
2 level tbsp plain flour
2 level tbsp spicy brown sauce
2 level tbsp dark brown sugar
1 level tsp made English mustard

Preheat the oven to 400°F/200°C/Gas Mk 6. Arrange the sliced onion in a dish. Mix the mince with the yoghurt and cornflour and season with salt and pepper. Divide into 4 equal portions. Toss in the flour and shape into oval beefburgers 3 x 2 in (7.5 x 5 cm). Place the beefburgers on top of the onion. Mix together the brown sauce, sugar and mustard and spread it over the beefburgers. Bake uncovered in the oven for 35 minutes. Serve the beefburgers with the onions in soft, buttered rolls.

CHILLI BEEF STIR-FRY
Serves 4

4 spring onions, sliced
4 tbsp dry sherry
1 inch (2.5 cm) piece root ginger, peeled and grated
2 tbsp chilli sauce
1 chilli, deseeded and finely chopped
1 lb (450 g) rump steak
1 tbsp oil
4 oz (110 g) mangetout
1 small can sweetcorn, drained

Mix together the spring onions, 1 tbsp sherry, ginger, 1 tbsp chilli sauce and the chilli in a bowl and season. Cut the steak in thin slices and mix with the marinade in the bowl. Stir well and leave for 30 minutes. Heat the oil in a large frying pan or wok and add the beef and marinade mixture. Cook over a high heat for 10 minutes, stirring continuously. Slice the mangetout lengthwise. Add to the pan and cook for 6 minutes. Mix together the remaining sherry and chilli sauce. Stir in together with the sweetcorn and cook for 1 minute. Serve with buttered noodles.

CHILLI CON CARNE
Serves 4

8 oz (225 g) tin kidney beans
2 tbsp oil
1 onion, chopped
1 red pepper, chopped
2 sticks celery, chopped
½-1 level tbsp chilli powder
1 lb (450 g) minced beef
8 oz (225 g) can tomatoes
¼ pint (150 ml) beef stock or water and beef stock cube

Heat the oil in a saucepan and fry the onion, pepper and celery very gently, stirring occasionally, until softened. Drain the beans, then add to the pan with all the other ingredients. Bring to the boil and simmer gently for about 30 minutes, stirring occasionally.

BASIC MINCED BEEF
Serves 6

1½ lbs (675 g) beef mince
1 large onion, chopped
2 cloves garlic, crushed
3 tbsp oil
small tin tomatoes
2 tsp tomato puree
¼ pint (150 ml) red wine
½ pint (300 ml) beef stock
3 heaped tsp cornflour
salt and freshly ground pepper
chopped parsley
pinch allspice

Soften the onion and garlic slowly in the hot oil in a large saucepan. Raise the heat and add the mince, turning it over and over to brown. Mix in the tomatoes, tomato puree, wine and half the stock. Bring to the boil, then lower the heat and simmer for about 15 minutes or until the meat is tender. Stir in the parsley and spice. Mix the cornflour with half the remaining stock and stir into the mince until well blended. Cook for a further 5 minutes. Add the remaining stock only if the mixture appears to be too dry. Serve with triangles of fried bread set round the edges.

STILTON STEAKS
Serves 4

4 oz (110 g) Stilton cheese, crumbled
1 oz (25 g) butter, softened
2-3 oz (50-75 g) shelled walnut pieces, finely chopped
pepper
4 sirloin steaks, each weighing approx 4-6 oz (110-175 g), trimmed

Mash the cheese in a bowl and add the butter and walnuts. Mix thoroughly. Place the steaks on a grill rack, adding pepper to taste. Place under a hot grill and cook for 2-10 minutes on each side, according to taste. Remove the steaks from the grill, sprinkle over the cheese and nut mixture pressing it down onto the meat. Put the steaks back under the hot grill and cook until the cheese has melted and is bubbling. Serve at once.

ORANGE MEATBALLS
Serves 4

1 lb (450 g) lean minced beef
1 medium onion, skinned and grated
grated rind of 1 orange
salt and freshly ground black pepper
1/4 tsp ground cinnamon
6 tbsp butter or margarine
2 tbsp butter or margarine
3 cups finely chopped raw spinach
1 cup finely chopped parsley
1 cup water
1 beef stock cube
1 cup orange juice
1/4 cup lemon juice
1 tbsp flour

Mix together the minced beef, grated onion, grated orange rind and ground cinnamon and season to taste. Shape into tiny balls between floured palms, and brown them all over in the 6 tbsp butter in a heavy-based saucepan. Remove and keep warm. Add the remaining 2 tbsp butter to the pan and, when it has melted, stir in the chopped spinach and parsley. Cook for about 10 minutes, stirring frequently. Return the meatballs to the pan, add the water and stock cube and simmer for about 15 minutes. Blend the flour with the orange and lemon juices, stir into the pan and simmer for another 20 minutes. Serve with buttered noodles, sprinkled with chopped parsley.

SIRLOIN STEAKS WITH MUSTARD
Serves 4

2 oz (50 g) English mustard
½ oz (10 g) plain flour
4 sirloin steaks, each weighing approx 6 oz (175 g)
2 tbsp fresh parsley, chopped
2 tbsp fresh thyme, chopped

Place the mustard and flour in a bowl and mix thoroughly. Spread over the top of each steak. Line a grill pan with foil, sprinkle over the herbs and place the steaks on top. Cook under a hot grill for 5-15 minutes, according to taste, turning the steaks frequently.

ITALIAN STYLE MEATBALLS
Serves 4

2 tbsp olive oil
1 large onion, skinned and finely chopped
2 garlic cloves, skinned and crushed
14 oz (400 g) can chopped tomatoes
2 tsp dried oregano
1 lb (450 g) minced beef
2 oz (50 g) fresh white breadcrumbs
2 oz (50 g) Parmesan cheese, freshly grated
1 egg, beaten
20 pitted black olives
vegetable oil, for deep-frying
4 fl oz (120 ml) dry red or white Italian wine

Heat the olive oil in a saucepan, add the onion and half the garlic and fry gently for about 5 minutes until soft. Add the tomatoes and half the oregano and season to taste. Bring to the boil, stirring, then lower the heat, cover and simmer for 20 minutes. Mix the mince with the breadcrumbs, Parmesan, remaining garlic and oregano. Season to taste and bind with the beaten egg. Pick up a small amount of the mixture about the size of a walnut. Press an olive into the centre, then shape the mixture around it. Repeat with the remaining olives and meat to make about 20 meatballs. Heat the oil in a deep-fryer to 375 F/190 C. Deep-fry the meatballs in batches for 2-3 minutes until browned, then drain thoroughly on kitchen paper. Stir the wine into the tomato sauce, then add ½ pint (300 ml) water and the meatballs. Shake the pan to coat the balls in the sauce, adding more water if necessary. Cover and simmer for 15 minutes, then check seasoning.

CRISPY MACARONI BEEF
Serves 4

4 oz (110 g) macaroni
1 tbsp oil
1 medium-sized leek, trimmed, washed and sliced
4 oz (110 g) carrot, chopped
1 garlic clove, crushed
12 oz (350 g) minced beef
4 oz (110 g) mushrooms, sliced
¼ pint (150 ml) beef stock
3 tbsp brown sauce

Topping:
2 oz (50 g) fresh breadcrumbs
2 oz (50 g) grated cheese
parsley to garnish

Cook the macaroni in boiling salted water as directed on the packet. Drain well. Heat the oil in a saucepan, add the leek, carrot and garlic and stir-fry for about 5 minutes to soften. Stir in the beef and cook, stirring, until brown. Mix in the mushrooms and stock and cook for a further 15 minutes. Add the brown sauce and macaroni, and season to taste. Pour into an ovenproof dish. Mix the breadcrumbs and cheese together and sprinkle over the top. Brown under a preheated moderate grill for about 10 minutes. Garnish with parsley.

ORANGE AND CRANBERRY MINCE
Serves 4

1 onion, chopped
1 tbsp oil
1 lb (450 g) lean minced beef
1 oz (25 g) plain flour
½ pint (300 ml) stock
1 tsp oregano
juice and grated rind of 1 orange
3 oz (75 g) cranberries

Heat the oil in a frying pan and cook the onion over low heat until soft. Add the meat, increase the heat and cook until browned. Stir in the flour, oregano, juice and rind of orange and stock. Cover and simmer for 20 minutes. Add the cranberries and simmer for a further 15 minutes until the meat is tender and the cranberries are soft but still whole.

MINCE HOT POT
Serves 6

1 tbsp oil
1 onion, chopped
1 lb (450 g) minced beef
8 oz (225 g) can tomatoes
8 oz (225 g) can baked beans
1/2 level tbsp plain flour
1/2 level tsp meat extract
1 lb (450 g) potatoes, thinly sliced
1 oz (25 g) margarine
3 oz (75 g) cheese, grated

Preheat the oven to 375°F/190°C/Gas Mk 5. Heat the oil in a frying pan and fry the onion and minced beef for 5 minutes, stirring occasionally. Stir in the can of tomatoes, the baked beans, flour and meat extract. Season to taste. Pour the mixture into a 1½ pint (900 ml) ovenproof dish. Arrange the potato slices on top of the meat, dot with margarine and bake in the oven for 30 minutes. Sprinkle with the cheese and return to the oven for 10 minutes.

BEEF AND BAMBOO SHOOTS
Serves 4

1½ lb (675 g) rump steak
1 lb (450 g) canned bamboo shoots, drained
4 tbsp oil
1 garlic clove, finely chopped
4 oz (110 g) carrots, thinly sliced
1 large onion, finely chopped
1 tsp ground ginger
1/2 tsp cayenne pepper
juice of 1 lemon
2 tbsp soy sauce

Cut the steak into thin slivers and slice the bamboo shoots. Melt the oil in a large frying pan or wok over high heat and add the garlic. When the garlic begins to sizzle, add the beef and carrots. Stir-fry until the meat is browned. Lower the heat and add the onion, bamboo shoots, ginger and cayenne pepper and stir-fry for 2 minutes. Pour in the lemon juice and soy sauce. Bring to the boil, stirring, then remove from the heat. Place on a warmed dish and serve immediately.

TURKISH MINCE
Serves 6

2 lb (900 g) lean minced beef
5 dessertspoons olive oil
4 tomatoes, peeled and sliced
1 large onion, peeled and grated
1 green pepper, deseeded and chopped
1 tsp grated nutmeg
½ clove garlic, crushed
1 tsp thyme
1 crushed bay leaf
2 tbsp tomato puree
½ glass red wine
1 beef stock cube
4 tbsp wholewheat flour
8 oz (225 g) Cheddar cheese, grated

Heat the oil in a large heavy-based saucepan, sauté the onions until soft, then add the mince and fry, turning, until browned. Add the green pepper and tomatoes. Cook for 10 minutes. Add the herbs, nutmeg, garlic and tomato puree. Stir and add the wine. Stir in the flour mixed to a paste with a little water. Cook gently for about 5 minutes and then add the crumbled stock cube and 1 cup of water. Simmer for 5 minutes, stirring constantly. Season to taste and add a little more water if necessary. Transfer to an ovenproof dish and sprinkle with the cheese. Put under a hot grill until the cheese bubbles.

STEAK DIANE
Serves 4

6 oz (175 g) unsalted butter
1 onion, finely chopped
4 rump steaks, each about 6 oz (175 g) in weight and about ¼ in (0.6 cm) thick
grated rind and juice of 1 large lemon
a few drops of Worcestershire sauce
2 tbsp brandy

Melt 2 oz (50 g) of the butter in a large, heavy frying pan, and fry the onion until soft. Remove the onion and keep warm. Add the remaining butter to the pan and fry the steaks for 1 minute on each side over high heat. Remove, place on a serving dish and keep warm. Return the onion to the pan. Stir in the lemon rind and juice and Worcestershire sauce. Add the brandy, ignite it and pour over the steaks. Serve as soon as the flames die down.

MEXICAN STEAK
Serves 4

4 oz (110 g) desiccated coconut
5 tbsp sunflower oil
1 large red onion, peeled and thinly sliced
2 cloves garlic, skinned and crushed
2 fresh green chillies, finely chopped
1 in (2.5 cm) piece fresh root ginger, peeled and grated
1 tsp turmeric
1 tsp cornflour
1 small green pepper and 1 small red pepper, deseeded and cut in strips
1 tsp sugar
4 x 8 oz (225 g) sirloin steaks, ¹/₂ in (1 cm) thick

Put the coconut in a bowl and pour 1 pint (600 ml) boiling water over it. Leave for 15 minutes. Sauté the onion, garlic, chillies, ginger and turmeric in 3 tbsp of the oil and fry gently for 3 minutes, stirring constantly. Strain the coconut through a sieve and add the juice to the pan. Bring to the boil. Lower the heat and simmer for 5 minutes. Blend the cornflour with 1 tbsp water, add to the pan and bring back to the boil. Add the pepper strips and cook for 5 minutes. Add the sugar and season to taste. Preheat the grill to a high heat. Brush the steaks with the remaining oil and season well. Grill for about 5 minutes on each side and serve with the sauce.

SCOTTISH STOVIES
Serves 4

12 oz (350 g) cooked beef
1 lb (450 g) potatoes
1 large onion
1 beef stock cube
about ¹/₂ pint (300 ml) hot water

Chop the cooked beef roughly. Peel and thinly slice the potatoes and onion. Fill a shallow pan with alternate layers of potato, meat and onion, seasoning each layer with salt and pepper. Finish with a layer of potatoes. Crumble the stock cube in the hot water and stir. Pour over the potatoes and cover with a lid. Simmer gently for 25-30 minutes, by which time the vegetables should be tender and most of the stock absorbed. However, if there is quite a lot of stock left, remove the lid, increase the heat and boil rapidly for 2-3 minutes.

STEAK CHASSEUR
Serves 4

4 x 8 oz (225 g) sirloin steaks
4 tbsp olive oil
1 garlic clove, finely chopped
2 oz (50 g) butter
12 oz (350 g) mushrooms, sliced
1 medium-sized onion, finely chopped
2 tbsp parsley, finely chopped
5 fl oz (150 ml) consommé
2½ fl oz (75 ml) Madeira or dry red wine mixed with 1 tbsp tomato puree and
1 tsp cornflour

Rub 2 tbsp oil and the garlic on the steaks. Sprinkle with pepper and leave for ½ hour. Melt half the butter with 1 tbsp oil in a frying pan over medium heat. Fry the steaks for 4 minutes on each side. Melt the remaining butter and oil in a separate frying pan. Add the mushrooms and sauté for 5 minutes. Add the onion and cook for one more minute. Remove the steaks from the pan, season to taste and keep warm. Add the consommé to this pan and boil to reduce by half. Add the wine and boil for 1 minute. Add the mushrooms, onion and parsley. Heat through, return the steaks to pan and serve immediately.

CHINESE BEEF STIR-FRY
Serves 4

1 lb (450 g) sirloin steak, trimmed
½ tbsp crushed black peppercorns
½ tsp mild chilli powder
3 tbsp soy sauce
3 tbsp dry sherry
1 tbsp sesame oil
8 oz (225 g) small cauliflower florets
2 x 7 oz (200 g) packets Chinese stir-fry vegetables
2 red chillies, deseeded and chopped
2 tbsp sesame seeds

Cut the steak into thin strips and marinade for about half an hour in a large bowl with the crushed peppercorns, chilli powder, soy sauce and sherry. Stir until it is evenly coated. Heat the oil in a wok or large frying pan, add the meat, reserving the marinade, and stir-fry for 5 minutes. Add the cauliflower florets and stir-fry for another 5 minutes. Add the Chinese vegetables, chillies and reserved marinade to the pan and stir-fry for 2 minutes. Serve immediately.

CABBAGE PARCELS
Serves 4

12 cabbage leaves
10 oz (300 g) minced beef
1 onion, peeled and chopped
2 tbsp tomato puree
1 tsp dried oregano
8 fl oz (240 ml) beef stock
3 oz (75 g) brown rice, cooked
1 oz (25 g) butter
1 oz (25 g) flour
3/4 pint (450 ml) milk
1/2 tsp allspice
4 oz (110 g) Red Leicester cheese, grated

Cook the cabbage in boiling water until tender. Dry-fry the mince until brown, drain off some fat, add the onion and sauté until soft. Stir in the oregano, tomato puree and stock, and cook until the liquid reduces by half. Stir in the rice. Heat the butter, flour and milk in a saucepan, stirring, until the sauce boils and thickens. Season with allspice and fold in the cheese. Spread out the cabbage leaves and place a spoonful of the mince stuffing on each. Fold the sides of the leaves to form parcels. Serve with the sauce and any remaining filling.

SWEET AND SOUR MEATBALLS
Serves 4

1 lb (450 g) minced beef
2 oz (50 g) onion, grated
1/2 tsp dried mixed herbs
2 tbsp oil
1 carrot, peeled and cut into small strips
3/4 pint (450 ml) beef stock
4 tbsp malt vinegar
3 oz (75 g) demerara sugar
4 tsp cornflour
1 tsp soy sauce

Mix the beef, onion and herbs together and season to taste. Form into 20 balls. Fry in the oil for 15-20 minutes and drain. Place the carrot, stock, vinegar and sugar in a saucepan and cook for 5 minutes. Blend the cornflour and soy sauce with a little water, stir in some of the hot stock from the saucepan, return to the pan and boil, stirring constantly. Place the meatballs on a serving dish and pour over the juice.

PORK

PORK CHOPS WITH CHEESE AND BEER
Serves 4

4 loin chops, each weighing approximately 6 oz (175 g)
4 oz (110 g) Cheddar cheese, grated
1 tsp prepared English mustard
3 tbsp brown ale
tomato halves and watercress sprigs to garnish

Cook the chops under a moderate grill for 7-10 minutes. Turn them over and cook for a further 7-10 minutes until cooked through. Place the cheese, mustard and ale in a bowl and mix well. Spread the mixture evenly over each chop and replace under the hot grill until the cheese has melted. Arrange the chops on a warm serving dish and garnish with the tomato and watercress. Serve at once.

PORK WITH PLUM SAUCE
Serves 4

1 lb (450 g) plums
1/2 pint (300 ml) rosé wine
salt and pepper
1 oz (25 g) plain wholemeal flour
1½ lb (675 g) pork fillet or tenderloin, trimmed and cubed
1 oz (25 g) butter
1 large onion, skinned and chopped
6 oz (175 g) white cabbage, shredded
2 tbsp natural yoghurt

Place the plums and wine in a saucepan and simmer gently for 5 minutes until tender. Strain and reserve the juice. Destone the plums and puree half the amount in a blender. Coat the pork cubes in the seasoned flour until well covered. Heat the butter in a large saucepan, add the onion and cabbage and cook gently for 3-4 minutes. Add the pork and fry until brown on all sides. Pour in the reserved plum juice and add the pureed plums. Simmer over low heat for 10-15 minutes until tender. Just before serving, add the remaining plums and yoghurt and reheat gently. Serve immediately.

OXFORD SAUSAGES
Makes about 18

2 lb (900 g) lean minced pork
12 oz (350 g) shredded suet
8 oz (225 g) fresh breadcrumbs
grated rind of half a lemon
1 tsp freshly grated nutmeg
1 tsp dried mixed herbs
pinch of dried sage
salt and pepper
1 lightly beaten egg
plain flour, to coat

Place the pork mince in a large bowl. Add the suet, breadcrumbs, lemon rind, nutmeg and herbs and mix thoroughly. Add salt and pepper to taste. Mix in the egg and stir vigorously with a fork until all the ingredients are well blended. Using lightly floured hands, form the meat mixture into sausage shapes and coat each in flour. Shake off any excess flour. Place the sausages under a hot grill and cook, turning frequently, until cooked through and browned on all sides.

PORK FILLET WITH MUSTARD CREAM SAUCE
Serves 4

1½ lb (675 g) pork fillet or tenderloin, cut into ½ in (1.25 cm) slices
½ oz (10 g) butter
1 tbsp vegetable oil
1 garlic clove, skinned and crushed
5 fl oz (150 ml) medium dry white wine
5 fl oz (150 ml) soured cream
2 tbsp mild wholegrain mustard
salt and pepper

Using a rolling pin or meat mallet, flatten the meat slightly. Melt the butter and oil in a frying pan over low heat, add the garlic and cook for 1 minute. Add the meat and cook until browned on both sides. Push the meat over to one side of the pan, then pour in the wine. Stir to loosen the sediment on the bottom of the pan and mix well with the wine. Add the soured cream and mustard. Bring the meat back from the side of the pan and mix it into the sauce. Cook for 3 minutes, stirring gently. Add salt and pepper to taste. Serve at once.

CIDER BACON CHOPS
Serves 4

4 bacon chops
1 tbsp English mustard
1 oz (25 g) demerara sugar
½ pint (300 ml) dry cider
½ oz (10 g) butter
2 tbsp plain flour
salt and pepper

Preheat the oven to 400°F/200°C/Gas Mk 6. Place the chops side by side in a large, ovenproof dish. Place the mustard and sugar in a bowl and use enough cider to blend to a smooth paste. Spread over the chops and leave for 30 minutes. Cook the chops in the oven for 15 minutes. In the meantime, put the butter, flour and remaining cider into a saucepan over low heat, whisking constantly until thick. Bring to the boil, lower heat and simmer for 2 minutes. Add salt and pepper to taste. Pour over the chops and cook for 15 minutes. Serve at once.

BACON ROSTI
Serves 4

2 lb (900 g) potatoes
1 onion, finely chopped
salt and freshly ground black pepper
2 tbsp olive oil
4 oz (110 g) spinach leaves, roughly shredded
8 rashers rindless back bacon

Finely grate the raw potatoes. Stir in the chopped onion and season well. Heat the oil in a large, heavy frying pan and fry the potato and onion mixture for 15 minutes, stirring continuously. Stir in the spinach. Reduce the heat and pat the mixture firmly into the base of the pan. Fry for a further 5 minutes. Grill the bacon rashers on each side until cooked. Chop the bacon rashers and sprinkle over the top of the rosti. Place under the grill again until crispy.

SWISS BACON CHOP
Serves 4

4 thick-cut smoked bacon chops
freshly ground black pepper
2 tsp ground sage
6 oz (175 g) tomatoes, sliced
5 oz (150 g) Gruyère cheese

Snip round the edges of the bacon chops with a pair of kitchen scissors to prevent them curling when grilled. Season to taste with freshly ground black pepper and grill for 2-3 minutes on each side until the fat starts to brown. Sprinkle half a teaspoon of ground sage on each chop and lay slices of tomato on top. Grate the Gruyère cheese over the chops. Grill again for 2-3 minutes until the tomatoes start to soften and the cheese turns golden. Serve with a fresh green salad.

CHEESY TOPPED GAMMON
Serves 4

4 x 6 oz (175 g) gammon rashers
a little melted butter
2 green eating apples
6 oz (175 g) Cheddar cheese, thinly sliced

Derind the gammon and snip each slice on the edge in a few places. Line the grill pan with foil and place the gammon slices in it side by side. Grill for 4-5 minutes, turning once. Wash and core the apple but do not peel. Slice thinly across in rounds and arrange over the gammon. Brush the butter over the apple and grill for 2-3 minutes. Place the cheese slices on the apple and grill for one more minute. Serve immediately.

BACON FRAIZE
Serves 4

8 eggs
3 tbsp single cream
1 oz (25 g) plain flour
8 oz (225 g) streaky bacon rashers

Place the eggs, cream and flour in a bowl and beat well to make a thin batter. Place the bacon under a hot grill and cook until just crisp. Lightly grease a frying pan, pour in half the batter and cook until the top is set. Place the bacon evenly on top. Pour over the remaining batter mixture and cook until set. Carefully turn over and cook until browned. Serve immediately.

BACON AND EGG SCRAMBLE
Serves 4

1 tbsp vegetable oil
1 medium-sized onion, finely chopped
8 slices of streaky bacon, coarsely chopped
4 courgettes, trimmed and chopped
2 large tomatoes, blanched, peeled and chopped
4 oz (110 g) button mushrooms, wiped clean and halved
½ tsp salt
¼ tsp pepper
6 eggs
4 tbsp milk
¼ tsp grated nutmeg
2 oz (50 g) fresh white breadcrumbs
1 tbsp butter, cut into small pieces

Heat the oil in a shallow, flameproof casserole over moderate heat. Add the onion and bacon, and cook, stirring occasionally, for 5 minutes until the onion is soft but not brown and the bacon is crisp. Stir in the courgettes, tomatoes, mushrooms and salt and pepper. Reduce to low heat and cook, stirring occasionally, for 15 minutes until the courgettes are tender. Remove the casserole from the heat and put aside. Mix together the eggs, milk and nutmeg in a bowl, then stir into the casserole. Return the casserole to low heat and cook, stirring constantly, until the egg mixture is nearly scrambled. Remove from the heat, sprinkle with breadcrumbs and dot the butter pieces on top. Place the casserole under a medium hot grill and cook for 3 minutes until the top is lightly browned. Serve immediately.

CHEESY BACON SLICE
Serves 4

2 tbsp olive oil
4 oz (110 g) rindless smoked back bacon, chopped
4 oz (110 g) button mushrooms, sliced
half bunch spring onions, finely sliced
6 eggs
4 oz (110 g) mature Cheddar cheese, grated
2 tbsp fresh parsley, chopped

Fry the bacon, mushrooms and spring onions gently in hot oil in a large frying pan for about 5 minutes. Beat the eggs and Cheddar together with the chopped parsley and season well. Pour over the bacon and mushroom mixture and cook over medium heat until the underside is golden and firm. Put the frying pan under a preheated grill and cook for a further 5 minutes or until the top is set. Cut into 4 wedges and serve with a crisp green salad, or new vegetables.

GLAZED GAMMON STEAKS
Serves 4

1 tbsp soy sauce
1/2 tsp mustard powder
1 tbsp golden syrup
1/4 tsp ground ginger
6 tbsp orange juice
garlic salt
black pepper
1 tbsp cornflour
1 tbsp lemon juice
4 gammon steaks

Place the soy sauce, mustard, syrup, ginger and orange juice in a small saucepan, adding garlic salt and black pepper to taste. In a small bowl, blend the cornflour and lemon juice together, also adding a little of the mixture from the saucepan. Pour this mixture into the saucepan and bring to the boil, stirring constantly. The mixture should thicken and glaze. Remove from the heat. Trim the gammon steaks if necessary and brush half of the glaze mixture onto one side of each steak. Place under a moderate grill and cook for 15 minutes, turning several times and continually brushing with the glaze. Serve at once.

BACON TURNOVERS
Serves 4

4 streaky bacon rashers, finely chopped
4 oz (110 g) self-raising flour
1 tsp mixed fresh herbs
¹/₂ tsp salt
5 tbsp milk

Place the bacon in a heavy-based frying pan and cook over low heat until the fat runs and bacon is just cooked. Remove the bacon with a slotted spoon and put aside, leaving the fat in the pan. Place the flour, herbs and salt in a bowl. Mix and pour in the milk, beating well to make a soft, firm dough. Place the dough on a flat floured surface, roll out to ¹/₄ in (¹/₂ cm) thick, then cut into eight 3 in (7.5 cm) rounds. Arrange the bacon evenly in the middle of four of the rounds, then cover with the remaining four rounds, pressing down firmly around the edges. Return to the frying pan and cook in the fat for 5 minutes until golden brown.

GERMAN PORK CHOPS
Serves 2

2 pork chops
¹/₄ onion, finely chopped
¹/₄ tsp parsley
¹/₄ tsp sage
¹/₂ beaten egg
breadcrumbs
1 oz (25 g) lard
8 oz (225 g) apples, peeled, cored and sliced
¹/₂ oz (10 g) margarine
1 oz (25 g) sugar
quarter lemon
2 tbsp white wine

Mix the beaten egg with the onion, parsley and sage. Dip the chops in seasoned flour, then in the egg mixture, then into the breadcrumbs. Press the breadcrumbs firmly onto the chops. Fry for 10-15 minutes on each side until well cooked. Put the sugar into a clean frying pan and melt, stirring all the time, then add the margarine, a squeeze of lemon juice and the wine. Add the sliced apple, cook gently until the apples are soft but not mushy and serve with the chops.

HUNGARIAN PORK FILLETS
Serves 4

4 pork fillets
2 oz (50 g) smoked bacon
1 onion, peeled and chopped
1½ green peppers, deseeded and chopped
1 smoked pork sausage, sliced
2 tsp tomato puree
1 tsp red paprika
pinch of chopped caraway seed
a little water

Fry the pork fillets quickly on both sides, remove from the pan and keep hot. Add the other ingredients in the order in which they are listed, frying each for a short while, then replace the pork fillets with the water. Simmer until tender. Serve with rice and a green salad.

BOOZY SAUSAGE CASSEROLE
Serves 2

8 oz (225 g) pork chipolata sausages
1½ oz (35 g) butter
2 oz (50 g) onion, skinned and finely sliced
4 oz (110 g) lean bacon rashers, derinded and diced
1 level tbsp flour
¼ pt (150 ml) chicken stock
2 tbsp dry white wine
4 oz (110 g) packet instant potato
boiling water
2 tbsp milk
chopped fresh parsley

Twist each chipolata into two and snip with scissors. Heat ½ oz (10 g) butter in a frying pan and sauté the chipolatas gently until brown all round, then remove from the pan and keep warm. Add the onion and bacon to the pan and fry for 3 minutes, stirring. Add the flour and stir well, then gradually blend in the stock and wine until smooth. Return the chipolatas to the pan, cover and simmer for 8 minutes. Make up the instant potato with the boiling water according to the instructions on the packet, season well and beat in the milk and remaining butter. Spoon into a forcing bag with a large nozzle and pipe around the edge of a flameproof serving dish. Place under a hot grill to brown slightly. Spoon the chipolatas and sauce into the centre and sprinkle with chopped parsley. Serve with green beans or peas.

BACONBURGERS
Serves 4

8 oz (225 g) cooked bacon
8 oz (225 g) pork sausagemeat
1 small onion, finely chopped
pinch of mixed fresh herbs
1 egg yolk
oil for frying

Mince the bacon and mix together with the sausagemeat. Place in a
bowl, add the onion, herbs and egg yolk and add salt and pepper to
taste. Mix thoroughly and divide into eight portions. Shape into flat
burger shapes and fry in hot oil for 6-8 minutes, turning over, until
well browned on both sides. Serve in hot baps.

EGG AND HAM FLORENTINE
Serves 4

1 lb (450 g) frozen leaf spinach, thawed
1½ oz (35 g) butter
1 oz (25 g) plain flour
¾ pt (450 ml) milk
pinch grated nutmeg
salt and freshly ground black pepper
3 oz (75 g) wafer thin sliced ham, chopped
8 size 4 eggs (4 larger eggs will be sufficient if preferred)
4 oz (110 g) Cheddar cheese, grated
2 tbsp fresh white breadcrumbs

Place the spinach in a saucepan and cook gently to extract all the
water and heat through. Drain thoroughly, pressing with the back of
a wooden spoon. Keep warm. Melt 1 oz (25 g) butter in another
saucepan and stir in the flour. Cook, stirring, for about 1 minute and
then gradually stir in the milk. Bring to the boil and cook, whisking,
until a smooth sauce is obtained. Season with the nutmeg and pepper
and salt. Stir one third of the sauce into the spinach and divide this
between four individual cocotte dishes. Lay the ham on top. Gently
poach the eggs and, making two wells in the spinach in each dish,
place the lightly poached eggs in these indentations. Stir half the grated cheese into the remaining white sauce and spoon over the eggs.
Sprinkle with the remaining cheese and breadcrumbs and flake a few
pieces of butter over the top. Place under a hot grill until golden
brown.

BROAD BEANS WITH SMOKED BACON
Serves 4

1 tbsp oil
1 onion, peeled and chopped
11 oz (325 g) smoked bacon, chopped
14 oz (400 g) broad beans, shelled
1/2 pt (300 ml) meat stock
salt
some ground paprika
1 tsp cornflour

Heat the oil in a pan, add the onion and cook for 5 minutes until soft.
Stir in the smoked bacon and the broad beans with salt and paprika to
taste. Pour in the stock, cover and simmer gently for 15-20 minutes
until the beans are tender. Mix the cornflour with sufficient water to
make a thin paste and gradually stir into the bacon and bean mixture.
Bring to the boil, stirring constantly, and cook for 2 minutes until
thick. Transfer to a warm dish and serve at once.

EGG AND BACON AU GRATIN
Serves 4

15 oz (425 g) can celery hearts, drained
4 rashers streaky bacon, derinded
4 hard-boiled eggs
4 oz (110 g) Cheddar cheese, grated
3/4 pt (450 ml) white sauce
mustard
4 slices white bread, crusts removed
butter, melted

Cut the celery hearts in thick slices and place in the base of a buttered
2 pt (1.1 ltr) casserole. Grill the bacon until crisp and chop it finely.
Halve the hard-boiled eggs lengthwise and remove the yolks. Cream
the chopped bacon and egg yolks together, press back into the cavities
in the egg whites and put the halves back together. Arrange on top of
the celery hearts. Stir about three quarters of the grated cheese into
the white sauce, together with a little mustard to give it a bite and
pour over the eggs. Dice the bread, dip into the melted butter and
scatter over the top of the dish. Sprinkle with the remaining cheese.
Place the dish under a low grill until the cheese begins to bubble and
the bread cubes are golden brown.

BACON ROLLS
Serves 4

6 rashers of back bacon
4 large bread rolls
oil for frying
6 oz (175 g) mushrooms, thinly sliced
3 oz (75 g) Cheddar cheese, grated
salt and pepper

Place the bacon under a hot grill and cook until crisp. Crumble the bacon. Slice the tops off the rolls, scoop out the middle and fry the bread from the inside of the rolls in the bacon fat in a frying pan until golden. Remove from the pan and, using a little oil, fry the mushrooms for 5 minutes. Place the bacon, mushrooms, fried crumbs and grated cheese in a bowl and mix well. Add salt and pepper to taste. Pile the mixture evenly into the four bread rolls and cook under a hot grill until browned.

SOMERSET CIDER GAMMON
Serves 4

4 gammon steaks
2 tsp made mustard
2 dessert apples, peeled and thinly sliced
¼ pt (150 ml) dry cider
pinch of fresh thyme
salt and pepper

Preheat the oven to 400°F/200°C/Gas Mk 6. Derind the gammon steaks. Spread mustard on both sides and place under a hot grill, cooking until both sides are browned. Cut four large squares of foil and place one gammon steak in the middle of each square. Arrange apple slices on top of the gammon. Pour any fat drippings from the grill pan over the gammon steaks. Pour on the cider and fold over the foil to make parcels. Arrange on a baking sheet and bake in the oven for 30 minutes. To serve, remove the steaks from the foil, arrange on serving plates and pour over the juices.

TANDOORI BACON CHOPS WITH RICE
Serves 4

half of a 4¹/₂ oz (120 g) packet of Indian savoury rice
¹/₂ small red pepper, seeded and diced
¹/₂ small yellow pepper, seeded and diced
4 bacon chops
1 tbsp tandoori paste

Cook the rice following the instructions on the packet, adding the diced peppers while the rice is cooking. Brush both sides of each bacon chop with tandoori paste and put under a preheated grill for about 5 minutes on each side or until cooked. Lay the chops on the plates and spoon the rice alongside. A crisp salad goes well with this dish.

ORIENTAL PORK AND PRAWNS
Serves 4

8 oz (225 g) vermicelli
1 tbsp vegetable oil
1 clove garlic, crushed
1 small onion, sliced
8 oz (225 g) pork tenderloin, thinly sliced
4 oz (110 g) peeled prawns
salt and pepper

Sauce:
2 tbsp light soy sauce
2 tbsp tomato ketchup
1 tsp lemon rind, finely grated
2 tbsp lemon juice

Cook the vermicelli according to the packet instructions. Drain well. In the meantime, heat the oil in a large frying pan, add the garlic and onion and cook, stirring, for 2 minutes. Add the pork, prawns and salt and pepper to taste and cook for 4 minutes until the pork is almost cooked. Place all the sauce ingredients in a bowl and mix well. Pour into the frying pan, together with the vermicelli. Cook for 2 minutes until the pork is cooked through. Arrange on a warm dish and serve at once.

PIQUANT BACON CHOPS
Serves 4

3 oz (75 g) butter, softened
1 tbsp fresh sage, chopped
1 1/2 tbsp creamed horseradish
squeeze of lemon juice
freshly ground black pepper
4 bacon chops

Put the softened butter in a bowl and stir in the chopped sage, creamed horseradish, lemon juice and black pepper. Mix together thoroughly and tip out onto a piece of greaseproof paper. Wrap the paper around the butter and roll into a sausage shape. Place in the freezer until hard. Heat the grill and grill the bacon chops for about 5 minutes on each side, or until cooked through. To serve, remove the butter roll from the freezer and cut into eight rounds; lay two slices on each bacon chop and serve with fresh new vegetables or a crisp green salad.

NORMANDY CASSEROLE
Serves 6

1 1/2 lb (675 g) pork sausages
1 large onion, peeled and sliced
1 tbsp fresh sage, chopped
1 tbsp fresh thyme, chopped
10 1/2 oz (310 g) can condensed tomato soup (or mushroom if preferred)
14 oz (400 g) can flageolet beans, drained
14 oz (400 g) can haricot beans, drained
14 oz (400 g) can butter beans, drained

Cook the sausages under a preheated grill, turning frequently until they are golden brown all over. Put a little oil or butter in the base of a large flameproof casserole and gently sauté the sliced onion until it is beginning to soften. Add the sausages, cut into chunks, together with the herbs. Pour in the tomato or mushroom soup and gently stir in the three tins of beans. Season to taste. Cover the casserole and simmer over a gentle heat for 20 minutes.

WELSH PORK CHOPS
Serves 4

4 pork loin chops, boned
4 oz (110 g) Emmental cheese, grated
6 pickled baby silverskin onions, halved
salt and freshly ground black pepper
1 tbsp fresh parsley, chopped

Grill the pork chops under a preheated grill for about 7 minutes on each side or until the fat around the meat begins to brown. Two minutes before the end of cooking time divide the cheese equally between the four chops, heaping it on top of each chop. Place the halved silverskin onions over the cheese and return to the grill. Grill until the cheese is bubbling, season well and sprinkle with parsley.

PICNIC TART
Serves 4

4 oz (110 g) shortcrust pastry
8 oz (225 g) pork sausage meat
1 tsp dried herbs
8 eggs
salt and freshly ground pepper
1¹/₂ oz (35 g) grated cheese

Preheat the oven to 400°F/200°C/Gas Mk 6. Line a 7 in (17.5 cm) square tin (or a sandwich tin) with the pastry. Trim the edges, flute them slightly and prick the bottom of the pastry case. Bake blind in the oven for 15 minutes. Mix the dried herbs with the sausage meat and shape into a roll. Press the sausage meat roll around the edges of the flan to form a border. Break the eggs inside the sausage meat border and sprinkle with seasoning. Cover with the cheese and bake for 30 minutes. Serve hot with vegetables or cold with salad.

HAM SCRAMBLE
Serves 4

2 large slices of bread, crusts removed
butter for frying
3 oz (75 g) cooked ham, finely chopped
2 eggs, beaten
1-2 tbsp milk
salt and pepper

Fry the bread in a little butter for about 3 minutes on each side until golden brown. Cut into triangles and keep warm. Add a little more butter to the pan and tip in the chopped ham, cooking gently for 2 minutes. Whisk the eggs, milk and seasoning together and pour into the pan over the ham. Stir over a gentle heat until the mixture begins to thicken and becomes creamy. Pile onto the bread and serve hot.

TUSCAN CASSEROLE
Serves 4

2 tbsp olive oil
4 streaky bacon rashers, rinded and diced
1 small onion, chopped
4 tbsp fresh parsley, chopped
2 tsp fresh basil, chopped
2 cloves garlic, crushed
14 oz (400 g) tin tomatoes
salt and freshly ground black pepper
7 oz (200 g) tin white haricot beans, drained

Heat the oil in a flameproof casserole and gently sauté the onion and garlic until they are beginning to soften, then add the bacon, parsley and basil and fry until the bacon is coloured. Add the tomatoes together with the juice and season to taste. Cover and simmer gently for 15 minutes. Tip in the drained beans, cover the pan again and simmer gently until the beans are heated through - about 10 minutes. Serve hot with crusty French bread and butter, or, for a more substantial meal, with rice.

LAMB

HONEY LAMB CHOPS
Serves 2

2 lamb chops
1 tbsp thick honey
1 tbsp oil
1 tsp lemon juice
½ tsp dried mixed herbs

Preheat the oven to 350°F/180°C/Gas Mk 4. Heat the honey, oil, lemon juice and herbs gently in a small saucepan until the honey has melted. Place the chops in a shallow, ovenproof dish, pour over the honey mixture and leave to stand in a cool place for 10 minutes. Cook in the oven for 20-25 minutes until the meat is tender and serve immediately.

SPANISH LAMB
Serves 4

2 tbsp olive oil
4 lamb chops, trimmed
1 small onion, peeled and sliced
1 aubergine, quartered and sliced
2 cloves garlic, peeled and crushed
15 oz (425 g) can green lentils, drained
15 oz (425 g) can chopped tomatoes
¼ pint (150 ml) chicken stock
½ tsp ground cinnamon
½ tsp grated nutmeg
salt and freshly ground black pepper

Fry the lamb chops in the hot oil until browned all over. Remove from the pan and add the onion and aubergine. Sauté for about 5 minutes until golden brown, stirring from time to time. Return the lamb chops to the pan together with the other ingredients and season well. Bring to the boil, cover the pan and allow to simmer gently for 25 minutes or until the lamb is tender. Serve on a bed of rice, noodles or couscous.

MUSTARD AND APPLE LAMB CHOPS
Serves 4

1 tbsp vegetable oil
1 onion, chopped
1 tomato, sliced
2 cloves garlic, crushed
8 lamb chops
2-3 tbsp Dijon mustard
8 fl oz (240 ml) apple juice
¼ pint (150 ml) chicken stock
black pepper

Heat the vegetable oil in a large frying pan. Add the onion, tomato
and garlic and fry for about 7 minutes until soft. Add the chops and
brown on both sides. In a bowl mix together the Dijon mustard,
apple juice and chicken stock. Season with pepper. Add to the pan
and stir well. Cover and cook for 15 minutes. Remove the lid and
cook on high heat for 10 minutes to reduce the sauce.

YORKSHIRE LAMB CUTLETS
Serves 4

4 lamb cutlets, trimmed
2 tbsp fresh breadcrumbs
salt and pepper
2 oz (50 g) Cheddar cheese, finely grated
2 oz (50 g) butter
4 onions, peeled and sliced
½ pint (300 ml) milk
1 oz (25 g) flour
2 tbsp fresh cream

Grill the cutlets on one side only. In a bowl, mix together the breadcrumbs, salt, pepper and cheese. Turn the cutlets over to the
uncooked side and spread the breadcrumb mixture over each one. Dot
1 oz (25 g) of the butter over the breadcrumbs. Continue to grill until
cooked. In the meantime, place the milk and onions in a saucepan and
boil. Lower the heat. Melt the remaining butter in a pan, stir in the
flour and cook over low heat for 1 minute. Remove from the heat and
stir in the milk and onion mixture. Return to heat and boil, stirring
constantly, until the sauce is thick. Stir in the cream. Place the cutlets
on a warm serving dish and pour over the sauce. Serve immediately.

TANGY LAMB CHOPS
Serves 4

2 tbsp vegetable oil
4 thick-cut lamb chops
salt and pepper
grated rind and juice of one lemon
2 tbsp chopped fresh parsley or 2 tsp dried
1 tbsp chopped fresh mint or 1 tsp dried
1 tsp sugar
1/4 pint (150 ml) stock

Heat the oil and fry the chops over high heat until browned all over. Lower the heat and season the chops with salt and pepper. Mix together the remaining ingredients. Spoon this over the chops and pour in the stock. Cover the pan and simmer gently for 30 minutes or until the meat is tender. Serve with the juices poured over.

BASIC MINCED LAMB
Serves 6

1 1/2 lb (675 g) lamb mince
1 large onion, chopped
2 cloves garlic, crushed
3 tbsp oil
2 tsp tomato puree
1/4 pint (150 ml) white wine
1/2 pint (300 ml) lamb stock
3 heaped tsp cornflour
salt and freshly ground pepper
chopped parsley
pinch coriander or rosemary

Soften the onion and garlic slowly in the hot oil in a large saucepan. Raise the heat and add the mince, turning it over and over to brown. Mix in the tomato puree, wine and half the stock. Bring to the boil, then lower the heat and simmer for about 15 minutes or until the meat is tender. Stir in the parsley and spice. Mix the cornflour with half the remaining stock and stir into the mince until well blended. Cook for a further 5 minutes. Add the remaining stock only if the mixture appears to be too dry. Serve with triangles of fried bread set round the edges.

GLAZED MINT CHOPS
Serves 4

4 lamb chops
mint jelly
4 large tomatoes, halved
sprigs of watercress or parsley to garnish

Heat the grill to moderate and remove the rack from the grill pan. Place the chops in the grill pan and spread 1 heaped teaspoon of mint jelly on each chop. Cook under the grill for 8-10 minutes, then turn the chops over and spread each one with another teaspoon of mint jelly. Add the halved tomatoes to the grill pan. Continue cooking for a further 8-10 minutes until the chops are tender and have a glaze. Watch the chops carefully, as the cooking time varies according to the thickness of the chops. Remove from the grill pan and arrange on a warm serving dish. Garnish with sprigs of watercress or parsley.

LAMB CHOP AND PLUM GRILL
Serves 4

8 small loin lamb chops
3 tbsp olive oil
pinch of cayenne pepper
12 oz (350 g) purple plums
1 large onion finely chopped
1 tbsp chopped thyme
5 fl oz (150 ml) dry white wine

Trim the fat off the chops. Brush oil over the chops and sprinkle cayenne pepper on both sides. Leave to stand for 15 minutes. Meanwhile stone and thinly slice the plums. Place the chops on the rack of a grill pan and cook under high heat for about 7 minutes on one side until they are brown. Turn the chops and grill for 1 minute more. Scatter the onion over the chops and contunue to grill until the onion begins to brown. Pour off any fat that has collected in the grill pan. Remove the rack and place the chops in the bottom of the pan. Arrange the plum slices over the chops, sprinkle with thyme and pour in the wine. Grill for 5 minutes or until they are cooked through.

ELY CHOPS
Serves 4

8 lamb chops
1 tbsp melted butter
salt and pepper
4 canned pear halves with their syrup
a little mint jelly

Brush the chops with butter and season with salt and pepper to taste.
Place under a moderate grill and cook until tender. In the meantime,
place the pears and a little of the syrup in a saucepan and warm gently. Drain. Put the chops on serving dish and arrange the pears around
them, placing a little of the mint jelly on top of each pear.

OXFORD STEAKS WITH CAPER SAUCE
Serves 4

4 lamb leg steaks, each weighing approx 6 oz (175 g)
salt and pepper
1 oz (25 g) butter
1 tsp plain flour
½ pint (300 ml) lamb or beef stock
2 tbsp drained capers
1 tbsp vinegar from the capers

Sprinkle the chops with salt and pepper to taste. Place the butter in a
frying pan, add the chops and fry over low heat for 10-15 minutes.
Turn over once to brown on both sides. Using a slotted spoon,
remove the chops from the pan and set aside on a warm dish. Loosen
any sediment left in the pan, then stir in the flour and cook for 2 minutes. Gradually pour in the stock and cook, stirring constantly, until
the sauce thickens, boils and is smooth. Mix in the capers, add the
vinegar and simmer over low heat for 2 minutes. Replace the chops in
the pan and simmer for 5 minutes until the lamb is cooked to taste.
Serve at once.

LAMB PAPRIKA-STYLE
Serves 6

1 oz (25 g) butter or margarine
8 oz (225 g) button mushrooms
½ pint (300 ml) tomato juice
2 level tsp paprika pepper
1 tsp Worcestershire sauce
6 lamb cutlets

Melt the butter or margarine in a large frying pan. Add the mushrooms and sprinkle with salt and pepper. Cook, stirring frequently, for 3 minutes. Add the tomato juice, paprika pepper and Worcestershire sauce. Bring to the boil and simmer for 10 minutes. Meanwhile, put the lamb cutlets in a grill pan, season with salt and pepper and grill for about 10 minutes or until tender, turning once. Place the meat on a serving dish and pour over the mushroom sauce.

LAMB AND APRICOT SAUTE
Serves 4

1 tbsp clear honey
1 tbsp soy sauce
½ tbsp whole mustard seeds (optional)
2 tsp English mustard
1 lb (450 g) lamb fillet, cut into cubes
12 dried apricots
2 tbsp oil
2 large potatoes, scrubbed and cut into sticks
2 leeks, sliced
8 oz (225 g) broccoli, divided into florets
1 tsp cornflour

Mix together the honey, soy sauce, mustard seeds (if using) and the mustard. Add the lamb and apricots then leave for a few minutes to marinate. Meanwhile, heat a tbsp of the oil in a large, non-stick frying pan, add the potatoes and cook gently, stirring occasionally, until they are soft. Heat the remaining oil in another pan. Add the meat and apricots, reserving any marinade, and stir-fry until the meat browns. Add the leeks and broccoli. Cover and cook for about 10 minutes until the meat and vegetables are tender. Mix in the potatoes. Transfer to a hot serving dish. Blend the cornflour into the reserved marinade then add to the pan juices. Heat, stirring, until thickened. Pour over the meat and vegetables and serve.

SHEPHERD'S PIE
Serves 4

2 lb (900 g) potatoes
2 oz (50g) butter or margarine
a little milk
2 tbsp oil
2 onions, chopped
1½ lb (675 g) shoulder of lamb, minced
1 level tbsp cornflour
¼ pint (150 ml) stock, or water and beef stock cube
1 tsp dried mint or 1 tsp cinnamon (optional)

Preheat the oven to 425°F/220°C/Gas Mk 7. Peel the potatoes and cook them in boiling, salted water until tender (about 20 minutes). Mash them well, ensuring that there are no lumps. Beat in the butter or margarine and sufficient milk to give a soft consistency. Heat the oil in a large saucepan and fry the chopped onion for about 3 minutes. Add the minced lamb, stirring to brown it all over. Blend the cornflour to a paste with a little of the stock. Add the remainder of the stock to the pan and season. Add the mint or cinnamon, if using. Cover the pan and simmer for 10 minutes. Stir in the blended cornflour and bring to the boil again. Turn the meat into an ovenproof dish. Cover with mashed potato and smooth the surface with a fork. Bake in the oven for 25 minutes or until the potato is well browned.

FILLET OF LAMB WITH REDCURRANT SAUCE
Serves 4

6 tbsp soured cream
1 garlic clove, skinned and crushed
1 tsp wholegrain mustard
1 lb (450 g) lamb fillet
2 tbsp dry red wine
1 tbsp redcurrant jelly

Preheat the oven to 350°F/180°C/Gas Mk 4. Mix the garlic and mustard with 2 tbsp of the soured cream. Season. Arrange the lamb in a roasting tin and spoon over the garlic mixture. Cook in the oven for 30 minutes until the lamb is tender. Transfer the meat to a warmed serving dish. Pour the wine into the roasting tin, stir to incorporate the sediment and add the redcurrant jelly. Bring to the boil, stir in the remaining soured cream and boil for 2-3 minutes until the sauce is quite thick. Cut the lamb into thick slices and spoon over the sauce.

MINT LAMB BURGERS AND CUCUMBER
Serves 4

1 lb (450 g) lean minced lamb
1 onion, peeled and chopped
4 oz (110 g) fresh breadcrumbs
grated rind of half lemon
3 tbsp fresh mint, chopped
1 beaten egg
2 tbsp plain flour
2 tbsp oil
half cucumber
6 spring onions, trimmed
7 fl oz (210 ml) stock
1 tbsp sherry

In a bowl, mix together the lamb, onion, lemon rind and breadcrumbs with 1 tbsp of mint. Add the egg and salt and pepper to taste. Shape the mixture into 12 balls, then press down to make flat burgers. Coat in flour. In a large frying pan, heat the oil and add the burgers. Cook until golden brown on both sides. Slice the cucumber into 2 in (5 cm) wedges and chop the spring onions. Add to the pan, pour in the stock and sherry and add the remaining mint and salt and pepper to taste. Bring to the boil, cover and simmer over low heat for 20 minutes.

LAMB FLORENTINE
Serves 4

8 lamb chops
1 oz (25 g) margarine
1 small onion, chopped
2 lb (1 kg) fresh spinach
¼ level tsp grated nutmeg
3 tbsp top-of-the-milk

Trim the chops of excess fat and put on a rack in the grill pan. Dot with half the margarine. Grill for 10 minutes, turning occasionally. Melt the remaining margarine in a large saucepan. Fry the onion until softened. Wash the spinach thoroughly and put it in the pan with the onion. Season to taste. Cover and cook very gently for 10 minutes until the spinach is cooked. Press the spinach and onion through a sieve or liquidise in a blender. Return the puree to the pan and stir in the nutmeg and the top-of-the-milk. Reheat. Pour the spinach mixture into a serving dish and arrange the chops on top.

PORTMANTEAU LAMB CHOPS
Serves 4

4 thick lamb loin chops
1½ oz (35 g) butter
4 oz (110 g) chicken livers, finely chopped
4 oz (110 g) mushrooms, finely chopped
1 beaten egg
2 oz (50 g) fresh wholemeal breadcrumbs
fresh parsley sprigs to garnish

Preheat the oven to 400°F/200°C/Gas Mk 6. Cut each chop horizontally working from the thick, outside edge to the bone, thus forming a pocket. Cook the chicken livers and mushrooms in ½ oz (10 g) melted butter in a frying pan for 5 minutes until soft but not browned. Add salt and pepper to taste. Remove from heat and allow to cool slightly before spooning the mixture into the pockets of the chops. Use wooden cocktail sticks to close the edges of the pocket. Dip the chops in the beaten egg and roll in the breadcrumbs until they are thoroughly coated. Arrange in a roasting tin. Melt the remaining butter and pour over the chops. Bake in the oven for 30 minutes, turning once.

LAMB CHOPS WITH RATATOUILLE
Serves 4

1 green pepper
1 red pepper
2 tbsp oil
1 large onion, sliced
1 clove garlic, crushed
4 thick-cut lamb chops
12 oz (350 g) courgettes, sliced
12 oz (350 g) tomatoes, peeled and quartered
salt and pepper

Remove the core and seeds from the peppers and cut into strips. Heat the oil in a saucepan and add the peppers, onion and garlic. Cover with a lid or foil and cook gently for about 15 minutes until soft but not brown. Meanwhile lightly fry the chops in a frying pan for about 10 minutes or until well browned on both sides. Add the courgettes and tomatoes to the saucepan with the salt and pepper and stir well. Arrange the chops on top and cook uncovered over gentle heat for about 15 minutes. Taste and check seasoning. Turn into a hot serving dish and serve immediately.

LAMB IN LEMON AND GARLIC
Serves 4

2 lemons
3 garlic cloves, crushed
8 lamb cutlets
4 tbsp oil
1 onion, peeled and finely chopped
6 fl oz (180 ml) natural yoghurt
¼ pint (150 ml) chicken stock
1 tsp fresh basil, chopped

In a bowl mix together the finely grated rind of 1½ lemons and the garlic and add pepper to taste. Blend well. Coat the lamb cutlets with the mixture and leave aside for 15 minutes. In a frying pan, heat the oil and cook the cutlets for 6 minutes, turning once, until the meat is tender. Remove with a slotted spoon, place on a serving dish and keep warm. Keep 2 tbsp of the fat from the pan and discard the remainder. Add the onion to the pan and cook until soft. Stir in the yoghurt and the juice of 1½ lemons. Add the basil and pour in the stock. Bring to the boil, then simmer over low heat for 2-3 minutes, seasoning to taste. Pour the mixture over the lamb cutlets and serve at once.

SPRING LAMB WITH VEGETABLES
Serves 4

4 lamb noisettes
1 tbsp oil
½ oz (10 g) butter
8 oz (225 g) cooked new potatoes, cut into thick slices
2 leeks, washed, trimmed and sliced
2 courgettes, sliced
2 tbsp redcurrant jelly
1 tbsp red wine

Heat the oil and butter in a large frying pan and add the potatoes, leeks and courgettes. Cook for 5 minutes, stirring all the time. Remove from the pan and keep on one side. Season the lamb with salt and pepper and place in the frying pan. Cook to seal for 5 minutes on each side. Mix together the redcurrant jelly and red wine and brush each side of the noisettes with this mixture. Return the potatoes, leeks and courgettes to the pan, cover with a lid and cook gently for a further 10 minutes or until the meat is cooked through and tender. Serve immediately.

ARABIAN MEATBALLS
Serves 4

1 onion, peeled and finely chopped
1 garlic clove, crushed
12 oz (350 g) minced lamb
1/2 tsp ground cinnamon
1/2 tsp ground cumin
3 tbsp fresh chopped marjoram or 3 tsp dried
15 oz (425 g) can chick peas, drained and mashed
1 egg, size 3, beaten
salt and freshly ground black pepper
oil for frying
1/2 pt (300 ml) natural yoghurt
8 oz (225 g) tagliatelle

Bring a large saucepan of salted water to the boil. Put the onion, garlic, lamb, spices, 1 tbsp marjoram and the chick peas in a bowl and mix together thoroughly. Beat in the egg and seasoning. Divide the mixture into 24 small balls, rolling the mixture between floured hands. Heat a little oil in a frying pan and fry the meatballs over a medium heat until browned. Stir in the yoghurt and remaining marjoram and simmer for 15 minutes, stirring from time to time. In a separate pan add the tagliatelle to boiling water with a little oil and cook for 10 minutes until just tender. Drain well and stir in a little butter. Arrange the tagliatelle on a warmed serving dish and spoon the meatballs and sauce over the top.

OFFAL

CHICKEN LIVER MASH
Serves 4

4 chicken livers
1 oz (25 g) butter
salt and pepper
3 tbsp Cheddar cheese, grated
2 tbsp cream
4 oz (110 g) potatoes, cooked and mashed
parsley

Preheat the oven to 425°F/220°C/Gas Mk 6. Place the washed and dried livers in an ovenproof dish. Top with butter and salt and pepper to taste. Cook in the oven for about 5 minutes. Remove from the oven, sprinkle over 2 tbsp of the cheese, the cream and the mashed potato. Sprinkle the remaining cheese on top. Put back into the oven and cook for a further 10-15 minutes until the top is golden brown.

IRISH KIDNEYS
Serves 4

8 lambs' kidneys
1½ oz (35 g) butter
1 medium-sized onion, skinned and chopped
2 canned red pimiento caps
salt and pepper
2 tbsp Irish whiskey
4 tbsp soured cream

Halve the kidneys, remove and discard the skin and cores, then cut into pieces. Melt the butter in a frying pan and cook the onion gently for 5 minutes until soft but not brown. Add the kidneys and cook for 10 minutes. Stir in the pimiento, salt and pepper to taste and simmer for a further 5 minutes. Pour over the whiskey and ignite. When the flames have died away, remove the pan from the heat, stir in the cream and reheat without boiling.

KIDNEYS AND BATTER
Serves 4

8 oz (225 g) plain flour
pinch of salt
2 eggs
1 pt (600 ml) milk
3 oz (75 g) butter
8 lambs' kidneys, skinned, decored and chopped
1 large onion, finely chopped
12 oz (350 g) mushrooms, finely chopped
1 garlic clove, crushed
2 glasses dry sherry
5 fl oz (150 ml) double cream
salt and pepper

Preheat the oven to 400°F/200°C/Gas Mk 6. Place the flour and salt in a bowl. Form a well in the centre, add the eggs and beat well. Gradually beat in the milk and whisk until smooth. In a frying pan, melt 2 oz (50 g) of the butter, add the onion and kidneys and cook gently until the onion is soft. Stir in the mushrooms, garlic and sherry. Heat gently for a few minutes, then stir in the cream. Simmer over low heat until the sauce is reduced and add salt and pepper to taste. Heat the remaining butter in an ovenproof dish. Pour in the batter, followed by the kidney mixture in the centre. Bake in the oven for 35 minutes until the batter has risen, and is golden and crisp. Serve at once.

PIQUANT KIDNEYS
Serves 4

1 lb (450 g) calves' kidneys
1 onion, peeled and finely chopped
2 oz (50 g) butter
2 tbsp parsley, chopped
1 tbsp wine vinegar
salt and pepper

Wash and trim the kidneys and cut into very thin slices. In a frying pan, heat the butter until melted and cook the onion and parsley for 5 minutes. Place the kidney slices in the pan and fry for 8-10 minutes, stirring from time to time. Pour in the vinegar, bring to boiling point, then remove from the heat. Add salt and pepper to taste and serve immediately.

KIDNEYS A L'ORANGE
Serves 4

4 rashers streaky bacon, without rinds and chopped
2 onions, peeled and thinly sliced
1½ oz (35 g) butter
8-10 lambs' kidneys, skinned, halved and cored
2 tbsp seasoned flour
½ tsp paprika
½ pt (300 ml) stock
finely grated rind and juice of 1 large orange
2 tsp tomato puree
orange wedges and chopped parsley to garnish

Fry the bacon and onions in the butter until soft. Roll the kidneys in the seasoned flour and add to the bacon and onions in the pan. Cook gently for 5 minutes, turning occasionally. Stir in the remaining flour and paprika, cooking for 1 minute, then gradually add the stock, orange rind and juice. Slowly bring to the boil, season to taste and add the tomato puree. Cover the pan and simmer for 20 minutes or until the kidneys are tender, adding more stock if necessary. Place on a warm serving dish, garnished with orange wedges and chopped parsley.

LIVER RAGOUT
Serves 4

1 lb (450 g) lambs' liver
4 level tbsp seasoned flour
1 onion, skinned and sliced
4 rashers of bacon, chopped
1 oz (25 g) fat or oil
¾ pt (450 ml) stock
1 oz (25 g) sultanas
1 apple, peeled and grated
1 level tsp tomato puree

Wash and trim the liver and cut it into small pieces. Dip it into the seasoned flour. Cook the liver, onion and bacon together in heated oil or fat in a frying pan until golden brown. Add the stock to the pan and bring to the boil, stirring constantly. Add the sultanas, apple and tomato puree. Lower the heat and simmer for 20 minutes.

PORTUGUESE KIDNEYS
Serves 4

8-10 lambs' kidneys
3 tbsp oil
2 onions, peeled and finely chopped
2 cloves of garlic, crushed
1 large red pepper, washed, deseeded and chopped
2 tbsp tomato puree
14 oz (400 g) can peeled tomatoes, chopped
4 tbsp beef stock or water
1-2 tsp Worcestershire sauce
dash of Tabasco sauce
1 tbsp lemon juice
1 oz (25 g) butter

Heat 2 tbsp of the oil in a pan. Add the onions and garlic and fry gently until soft. Add the red pepper and cook gently for 5 minutes. Stir in the tomato puree, tomatoes, stock, Worcestershire sauce, Tabasco and lemon juice, season to taste and bring to the boil. Cover the pan and simmer for 15 minutes, stirring occasionally. Meanwhile, heat the remaining oil and butter in another pan. Add the kidneys and fry gently for 10 minutes, turning them over from time to time until they are almost cooked. Add the tomato mixture and simmer for 10 minutes.

LIVER WITH SAGE AND MADEIRA SAUCE
Serves 4

1 lb (450 g) lambs' liver, sliced
1½ tbsp flour
½ tsp dried sage
1½ oz (35 g) butter
15-20 fresh sage leaves
4 tbsp chicken stock
4 tbsp Madeira
few sprigs of sage to garnish

Cut the sliced liver into very thin strips. Mix together the flour and dried sage in a bowl and season to taste. Dip the liver strips into the flour. Fry the liver in heated butter for 2 minutes, turning the meat until it is brown on both sides. Add the sage leaves and continue to cook the liver, turning occasionally, for 1-2 minutes longer, until it is just cooked. Pour in the stock and Madeira, stir to mix with all the pan juices and bring to the boil. Adjust seasoning if necessary. Place the liver and sauce on a serving dish and garnish with sage.

KIDNEYS JEREZ
Serves 4

1 lb (450 g) lambs' kidneys
1 tbsp plain flour
1/2 oz (10 g) butter
1 small onion, finely chopped
1/4 pt (150 ml) single cream
4 tbsp dry sherry
salt and pepper
2 tbsp chopped fresh parsley to garnish

Wipe the kidneys and cut in half. Cut out the stringy centre pieces and cut in half again. Coat with flour. Sauté the onions gently in the melted butter for 1 minute and then add the kidneys. Cook gently for 10 minutes, or until the kidneys are cooked through and no blood runs out. Stir in the sherry and bring to the boil. Season well and pour in the cream. Heat through and serve sprinkled with chopped parsley on a bed of cooked rice.

LIVER AND BEANS
Serves 4

2 tsp oil
2 onions, peeled and sliced
1 green pepper, deseeded and sliced
1 lb (450 g) lambs' liver
1 x 15 oz (425 g) can of baked beans
3 oz (75 g) pasta shapes
1/2 pt (300 ml) stock
1 tbsp Worcestershire sauce
2 tbsp vinegar
pinch of mixed dried herbs
5 fl oz (150 ml) natural yoghurt

In a saucepan, heat the oil and gently cook the onion for 1 minute. Add the green pepper, cover and cook over low heat for 3-4 minutes. Slice the liver into strips and add to the onion in the saucepan. Mix in the beans, pasta, Worcestershire sauce, vinegar and herbs and pour in the stock. Cover and simmer for 15-20 minutes, stirring from time to time to prevent the mixture from sticking to the saucepan. Remove from the heat and stir in the yoghurt to serve.

EGG, LIVER AND MUSHROOM BAKE
Serves 4

1 oz (25 g) butter
1 onion, finely chopped
4 slices of lean bacon, diced
8 oz (225 g) chicken livers, roughly chopped
4 oz (110 g) button mushrooms, wiped clean and halved
2 tbsp tomato puree
1/2 tsp salt
1/4 tsp pepper
4 eggs
2 oz (50 g) Cheddar cheese, finely grated

Preheat the oven to 375°F/190°C/Gas Mk 5. Using half the butter, grease four ramekin dishes. In a small frying pan melt the remaining butter over low heat. When the foam subsides, add the onion and bacon and cook for 5 minutes. Add the chicken livers and mushrooms and cook for a further 5 minutes until the livers are lightly browned, the bacon is crisp and the onion and mushrooms are soft. Remove the pan from the heat and drain off the excess fat. Stir the tomato puree, salt and pepper into the pan. Divide the liver mixture into four equal amounts and place in each ramekin. Break an egg on top of each one, then sprinkle over the cheese. Bake in the oven for 15-20 minutes, or until the eggs are set and the cheese is lightly browned. Serve immediately.

LIVER AND ONIONS

1 1/2 lb (675 g) onions, peeled and sliced
6 slices of lamb's liver, trimmed and wiped
salt and pepper
3 tbsp plain flour
3 oz (75 g) butter
2 tbsp parsley, chopped

In a bowl, mix the flour with salt and pepper to taste. Dip in the liver slices until they are well coated. Melt the butter in a large frying pan. Add the onions and cook until golden. Add the liver slices and cook for 3 minutes on each side. Mix in the chopped parsley. Place the liver and onions on a warm serving dish and pour over the juices from the pan.

ORIENTAL KIDNEYS
Serves 4

1 lb (450 g) ox kidney
1 tbsp vegetable oil
½ pt (300 ml) dry ginger ale
2 tsp malt vinegar
1 oz (25 g) butter
4 oz (110 g) mushrooms, washed and sliced
1 oz (25 g) flaked almonds
1 oz (25 g) sultanas
1 tbsp gravy powder
3 tbsp cold water

Cut the kidney into slices about ¾ in (2 cm) thick. Remove the core and chop the slices. Fry in heated vegetable oil in a saucepan, turning occasionally, until it is lightly browned all over. Add the ginger ale and vinegar, season to taste and bring to the boil. Lower the heat and simmer, covered, for 30 minutes. In the meantime, melt the butter in a frying pan, and cook the sliced mushrooms for 3 minutes, turning frequently. Add the mushrooms, almonds and sultanas to the kidney mixture, stir well and simmer for 10 minutes. Mix the gravy powder with cold water until smooth, and then stir into the kidney mixture. Bring to the boil, stirring constantly. Lower the heat and simmer for 5 minutes. Serve at once.

BAKED LIVER DUMPLINGS
Serves 4

4 oz (110 g) self-raising flour
2 oz (50 g) shredded suet
1 level tsp dried sage
6 oz (175 g) lambs' liver
1 oz (25 g) beef dripping

Preheat the oven to 375°F/190°C/Gas Mk 5. Place the flour, suet and sage in a bowl and season with salt and pepper. Slice the liver into thin strips and then dice into small cubes about ¼ in (0.6 cm) square. Add to the bowl. Beat together the egg and 1 tbsp water and add, stirring all the ingredients together to make a stiff mixture. Place a little beef dripping in the bottom of 8 bun tins and heat in the oven until melted. Divide the mixture equally between the bun tins and cook in the oven for about 25 minutes until crisp and lightly browned. Serve hot.

LIVER IN COINTREAU
Serves 4

4 x 6 oz (175 g) liver, sliced
2 oz (50 g) flour
1 tsp dried marjoram
2½ fl oz (75 ml) oil
2 onions, chopped
4 fl oz (120 ml) red wine
1 fl oz (30 ml) orange juice
2 tbsp Cointreau
1 tbsp brandy

Mix together the flour and marjoram and add salt and pepper to taste. Dip the liver into the flour and shake off any excess flour. Reserve 1 tbsp of the flour. Heat the oil in a frying pan and cook the onions until soft. Remove and drain. Place the liver in the pan and cook on both sides for 4 minutes, then set aside on a warm serving dish. Gradually whisk the wine, reserved flour, orange juice, Cointreau and brandy into the pan, then add the onions. Continue to stir over low heat until the sauce thickens. Pour over the liver and serve hot.

WELSH LIVER
Serves 4

1 tbsp sesame seeds
2 tbsp vegetable oil
1 in (2.5 cm) root ginger, sliced thinly
2 cloves garlic, peeled and sliced thinly
1½ lb (675 g) lambs' liver
8 spring onions, washed and trimmed
2 leeks, washed and sliced
2 tbsp clear honey
1 tbsp light soy sauce
half orange, juice and grated rind

Dry-fry the sesame seeds in a large frying pan until golden (about 1 minute). Set on one side. Heat the oil and fry the ginger and garlic for 2 minutes without burning. Add the liver and cook to seal for 2 minutes. Add the spring onions and leeks and cook for another 2 minutes on slightly lower heat. Mix together the honey, soy sauce and orange juice, season and pour into the pan. Cook for a further 2 minutes. Serve on a bed of cooked rice sprinkled with the sesame seeds and orange rind.

LIVER AND SATSUMAS
Serves 4

2 satsumas
1 lb (450 g) lambs' liver
2 tbsp plain flour
pepper
2 tbsp oil
1 onion, peeled and sliced
2 tbsp fresh parsley, chopped

Derind the satsumas and cut the rind into very thin strips. Divide the satsumas into segments. Slice the liver into strips. Mix the flour and pepper together in a bowl and dip in the liver strips until well coated. Heat the oil in a pan, add the onion and gently cook until soft. Add the liver and cook, stirring from time to time, for 5 minutes until the liver changes colour. Add the satsuma segments and parsley and cook for 2 minutes until the fruit has softened slightly and the liver is tender. Garnish with the satsuma rind and serve at once.

KIDNEY TOASTS
Serves 2

8 oz (225 g) calf's kidney or 4 lamb's kidneys
4 oz (110 g) mushrooms, wiped and sliced
2 oz (50 g) butter
1 oz (25 g) flour
1/2 pt (300 ml) stock
4 tbsp single cream
1 tbsp dry sherry
2 large slices white bread
butter
salt and pepper
chopped fresh parsley

Remove the fat and skin from the kidneys and remove the core. Cut into small pieces and sauté in the melted butter for about 3 minutes. Add the sliced mushrooms and continue cooking gently for another 3 minutes. Stir in the flour and mix well. Gradually add the stock, stirring until it has thickened. Bring to the boil, reduce the heat, cover and simmer very gently for about 20 minutes or until the kidney is cooked. Stir in the sherry, season to taste and add the cream, taking care not to boil the mixture. Toast the bread slices, butter them and spoon the mixture onto the toast. Sprinkle with the chopped parsley.

LIVER ITALIANO
Serves 4

12 oz (350 g) lambs' liver
salt and freshly ground black pepper
1 oz (25 g) plain flour
1½ oz (35 g) butter
1 lb (450 g) onions, thinly sliced
¼ pt (150 ml) beef stock
½ pt (300 ml) milk
2 tbsp tomato puree
1 clove garlic, finely chopped
¼ tsp dried mixed herbs
2 tbsp double cream
chopped parsley

Cut the liver into bite-sized pieces. Season the flour and coat the liver pieces, then fry them in the melted butter until browned all over. Remove from the pan and put on one side. Sauté the onions and garlic in the butter until soft. Tip any remaining flour into the pan and stir in. Cook for 1 minute. Gradually stir in the stock, milk, tomato puree, and herbs. Bring to the boil, stirring, and cook for a few minutes. Add the liver, cover the pan and cook very gently for 10-15 minutes or until the liver is tender. Season to taste. Pour the liver and sauce into a warm serving dish, pour the cream over the top and sprinkle with chopped parsley.

POULTRY

CHICKEN BREASTS WITH CINNAMON
Serves 4

4 chicken breasts
2 tbsp flour
2 oz (50 g) butter
1 medium-sized onion
1 tsp cinnamon
2 cloves
3½ fl oz (100 ml) white wine vinegar
4 tbsp double cream

Peel the onion and chop finely. Cut each chicken breast in half lengthwise and flatten with a knife blade. Sprinkle a little flour on each side of chicken. Add the onion and chicken to the melted butter in a frying pan and brown lightly over medium heat. Add the vinegar, cloves, cinnamon and salt and pepper to taste, and, when the vinegar has completely evaporated, pour in the cream. Cover and simmer over a low heat for 15 minutes, turning occasionally with a wooden spatula.

NORMANDY CHICKEN
Serves 4

2 fl oz (60 ml) vegetable oil
1 x 3 lb (1.3 kg) chicken, cut into pieces
1 onion, chopped
1 clove garlic, crushed
3 streaky bacon slices, chopped
1 oz (25 g) flour
15 fl oz (450 ml) dry cider
2 red apples, cored and chopped
5 fl oz (150 ml) double cream

Fry the chicken pieces in the oil until evenly browned. Transfer to a plate and keep warm. Add the onion, garlic and bacon to the pan and cook for 5 minutes, stirring from time to time. Stir in the flour to form a smooth paste and gradually stir in the cider. Bring to the boil and simmer for 3 minutes. Return the chicken pieces to the sauce and simmer for 30 minutes or until the chicken is cooked through. Add the apples and cream and cook gently for 5 minutes. Do not let it boil.

POULTRY LOAVES
Serves 4

8 oz (225 g) cooked, minced poultry meat
1/2 pt (300 ml) thick white sauce
2 beaten eggs
pinch mixed herbs
salt and freshly ground black pepper

Preheat the oven to 350°F/180°C/Gas Mk 4. Mix all the ingredients well and pack into buttered individual loaf tins. Cover each one with buttered paper. Stand in a bain-marie and cook gently for 30 minutes or until well set. Turn out the loaves and leave to cool. Serve with a crisp salad and slices of tomato.

CHICKEN JULIENNE
Serves 4

1 lb (450 g) cooked chicken meat
half red pepper and half yellow pepper, deseeded
6 oz (175 g) mangetout
1 1/2 oz (35 g) butter
1 1/2 oz (35 g) flour
1/2 pt (300 ml) rich chicken stock
1/2 pt (300 ml) milk
2 tbsp lemon juice
1 oz (25 g) Cheddar cheese, grated
pinch dried rosemary
salt and freshly ground pepper
1-2 tbsp chopped parsley

Place the halves of pepper under the grill until the skins are black and blistered, then remove the skins and cut the peppers into strips. Cut the cooked chicken into equal sized strips. Blanch the mangetout in boiling, salted water for about 3 minutes, then drain. Melt the butter in a pan and stir in the flour. Cook gently, stirring, for a few minutes and then gradually add the chicken stock and milk, stirring well to prevent lumps from forming. Bring the sauce to the boil, then simmer for about 3 minutes. Add the lemon juice, cheese and rosemary. Season to taste. Add the chicken, peppers and mangetout and simmer gently for a few minutes to heat through. Serve on a bed of rice sprinkled with chopped parsley.

DEVILLED CHICKEN
Serves 4

4 joints of cooked poultry

Dressing:
pinch Cayenne pepper
1/2 tsp freshly ground black pepper
1 tsp Worcestershire sauce
1 tsp made mustard
1 tsp vinegar
1 tbsp salad oil

Mix together all the dressing ingredients. Cut the chicken into neat pieces, removing the skin, and brush with the devil sauce dressing. Put the chicken under a hot grill and cook quickly until it is well browned, turning the chicken pieces frequently while cooking. Serve with a crisp green salad for a quick and easy snack.

CHICKEN BREASTS IN PORT
Serves 4

4 chicken breasts
1 clove garlic, chopped
2 small onions, peeled and finely sliced
2 oz (50 g) butter
1/2 pint (300 ml) chicken stock
1/4 pint (150 ml) port wine
4 oz (110 g) mushrooms, wiped and sliced
salt and freshly ground pepper
chopped parsley to garnish

Slice the chicken breasts into 1/2 inch (1.25 cm) thick slices and lightly dust them with seasoned flour. Gently sauté the finely sliced onions and chopped garlic in the melted butter until golden brown. Remove with a slotted spoon, drain and keep warm. Fry the chicken breasts on both sides until lightly browned and then return the onions and garlic to the pan. Add the chicken stock, port wine and mushrooms, bring to the boil, then turn the heat down, cover the pan and simmer very gently for 15 minutes. Season to taste and serve garnished with the chopped parsley.

CHICKEN COCOTTES
Serves 4

4 oz (110 g) cooked chicken, minced
2 mushrooms, finely chopped
2 eggs, separated
2 tbsp single cream
salt and freshly ground pepper
¹/₂ oz (10 g) butter

Preheat the oven to 350°F/180°C/Gas Mk 4. Mix the chicken and mushrooms and bind with the egg yolks and cream. Season well. Whisk the egg whites stiffly and fold into the chicken mixture. Divide between 4 buttered ramekins, place them on a baking tray and cook in the centre of a preheated oven for 15-20 minutes.

CARIBBEAN CHICKEN
Serves 4

6 jointed chicken legs
salt and pepper
4 tbsp oil
12 oz (350 g) can pineapple pieces
1 red pepper
1 green pepper
2 tsp soy sauce
2 tsp Worcestershire sauce
1 tsp arrowroot or cornflour

Season the chicken pieces and fry gently in the hot oil for about 10 minutes, turning over during cooking. Remove from the pan and keep warm. Deseed the peppers and cut the flesh into strips. Fry gently in the remaining oil until soft. Return the chicken to the pan, drain the pineapple, reserving the juice, and add to the pan together with the soy and Worcestershire sauce. Mix the arrowroot with a little of the juice until smooth, stir in the remaining juice and add to the pan. Bring to the boil and cook, stirring, until slightly thickened. Cook gently for 20 minutes, stirring occasionally. Arrange the chicken on a warmed serving plate and pour the sauce over. Serve hot with rice.

CHICKEN CACCIATORE
Serves 6

1 tbsp oil
3 lb (1.3 kg) chicken
14 oz (400 g) can tomatoes
4 fl oz (120 ml) red wine
1 clove garlic, crushed
1 tsp basil, chopped
salt and pepper
12 small white onions, peeled
2 large green peppers, cut into strips
1 tbsp cornflour
1 tbsp water

Brown the chicken pieces all over in the hot oil. Stir in the tomatoes, their juices, the wine, garlic, basil and seasonings. Bring to the boil, then lower the heat and simmer gently for 15 minutes. Add the onions and green peppers, cover and simmer for another 15 minutes or until the vegetables are tender and the chicken is well cooked. Mix the cornflour with a little water and gradually stir into the chicken mixture. Cook for another 5 minutes or until the gravy has thickened.

CHICKEN AND SWEETCORN
Serves 4

4 chicken joints
3 oz (75 g) butter
1 bunch spring onions, trimmed and sliced diagonally
1 can new potatoes, drained and sliced
1 can sweetcorn, drained
1 oz (25 g) flour
1/2 pt (300 ml) milk
salt and pepper
few sprigs of fresh parsley

Melt 2 oz (50 g) of the butter in a frying pan with a little oil and fry the chicken joints until they are brown all over, which should take about 20 minutes. Sauté the sliced spring onions and potatoes in the remaining butter, add the sweetcorn and mix well. Stir in the flour and cook for a further 3 minutes. Gradually stir in the milk, bring to the boil and cook until thickened (about 5 minutes), stirring all the time. Season well. Pour the mixture into a shallow dish and arrange the chicken on top of the sauce. Garnish with parsley sprigs.

SAUTE CHICKEN
Serves 4

2 large chicken breasts, cut in half
1½ tbsp cooking oil
2 oz (50 g) chopped onions
4 oz (110 g) sliced mushrooms
4 tbsp dry white wine
salt and pepper
white seedless grapes to garnish

Season the chicken breasts with salt and papper and sauté in the oil until lightly browned. Add the onions, mushrooms and white wine. Cover and cook on low heat for about 30-40 minutes, or until the chicken is tender. Serve with the sauce from the pan and garnish with grapes.

CHICKEN JEREZ
Serves 4

4 chicken joints
salt and black pepper
4 oz (110 g) butter
4 oz (110 g) button mushrooms
1 oz (25 g) plain flour
2 tbsp sherry
½ pt (300 ml) chicken stock
¼ pt (150 ml) single cream
few slices of white bread
oil and butter for frying
2 sprigs fresh parsley

Season the chicken well with salt and pepper and fry gently for 25 minutes, turning from time to time. Remove and keep hot. Add the mushrooms, whole, and cook them for about 4 minutes. Remove and keep to one side. Stir the flour into the remaining fat, and cook gently for 3 minutes. Gradually stir in the sherry and stock, whisking to prevent lumps from forming. Bring to the boil and cook until thickened, stirring all the time. Stir in the cream and mushrooms, and reheat gently making sure the sauce does not boil. Cut out shapes from the bread slices with small cutters. Fry in hot oil and butter until crisp and golden. Pour the chicken into a warm serving dish and decorate with the fried croutons and parsley sprigs.

MUSTARD CHICKEN
Serves 4

4 chicken breasts
3 oz (75 g) butter
1 tbsp oil
3-4 tbsp Dijon mustard
2 tbsp chopped spring onions
¼ tsp thyme
salt and freshly ground pepper
pinch of cayenne pepper

Brush the chicken breasts with melted butter and grill for 10 minutes on each side, brushing regularly with the butter and oil. Blend together the mustard, spring onions, thyme, and seasoning and slowly add to the rest of the oil and butter mixture, to thicken it. Spread some of the mixture on to the skin side of the chicken and cook gently for another 10 minutes or until it is golden brown and tender, basting with the marinade from time to time.

SPANISH CHICKEN
Serves 4

4 chicken joints
salt and black pepper
3 tbsp oil
4 large tomatoes, skinned and chopped
1 clove garlic, peeled and crushed
½ tsp each fresh thyme and basil
¼ pt (150 ml) white wine
12 black olives
1 tsp fresh parsley, chopped

Preheat the oven to 350°F/180°C/Gas Mk 4. Season the chicken joints well and fry in the hot oil for 20 minutes, turning from time to time. Transfer to an ovenproof dish, cover and continue to cook in a preheated oven for a further 10 minutes. Fry the tomatoes and garlic in the remaining oil, and add the herbs and wine. Bring to the boil and cook gently until soft. Add the olives and mix well. Arrange the chicken on a warm serving dish, pour the sauce over and sprinkle with chopped parsley. Serve with a crisp green salad.

HAM WRAPPED CHICKEN
Serves 4

4 chicken breasts, skinned and boned
4 large slices Parma ham
4 oz (110 g) Gruyère cheese, grated
2 oz (50 g) unsalted butter
6 tbsp chicken stock
6 tbsp dry white wine
1 tbsp double cream
sprinkling of paprika

Preheat the oven to 350°F/180°C/Gas Mk 4. Carefully flatten the chicken breasts with a rolling pin and lay each one on a slice of ham. Sprinkle over half the cheese, roll up and secure with a cocktail stick. Melt the butter in a pan, brown the chicken and then place it in a casserole dish. Add the stock and wine to the frying pan and boil until reduced. Pour over the chicken and then pour the cream on top. Cover with the remaining cheese and sprinkle with paprika. Cover and bake for 25-30 minutes.

GINGERED JAPANESE CHICKEN
Serves 4

1 x 3 lb (1.3 kg) oven-ready chicken
1 tbsp plain flour
1 tbsp ground ginger
4 tbsp vegetable oil
1 onion, skinned and sliced
10 oz (300 g) can bamboo shoots
1 red pepper, halved, seeded and sliced
1/4 pint (150 ml) chicken stock
3 tbsp soy sauce
3 tbsp medium dry sherry
4 oz (110 g) mushrooms, sliced

Cut all the flesh off the chicken and slice into chunky fingers, discarding the skin. Mix the flour and ginger together in a polythene bag and toss the chicken in it to coat. Heat the oil in a large, deep frying pan and fry the chicken and sliced onion together for 10-15 minutes until they are both golden. Cut up the canned bamboo shoots into 1/2 inch (1 cm) strips and add to the pan, together with the sliced pepper. Then stir in the stock, soy sauce and sherry and season. Bring to the boil, cover and simmer for 15 minutes. Add the sliced mushrooms, cover again and cook for a further 5 minutes.

BREAST OF CHICKEN WITH WALNUT SAUCE
Serves 4-6

4-6 chicken breasts
seasoned flour
2 oz (50 g) butter
1 tbsp oil
4 tbsp Calvados or brandy
12 fl oz (350 ml) dry cider
8 fl oz (240 ml) single cream
2 tbsp chopped walnuts
2 large green apples, cut into wedges

Cut the chicken breasts in half and dust with seasoned flour. Heat the butter and oil in a large pan with a tight-fitting lid. Brown the breasts on each side, and season with salt and pepper. Meanwhile heat the Calvados or brandy in a small pan, set alight and pour over the chicken. Shake the pan until the flames subside and then pour in the cider. Cover and simmer gently for 5 minutes, or until the breasts are cooked and tender. Remove and keep warm. Boil the liquid in the pan rapidly to reduce by half. Taste, adjust the seasoning and stir in the cream and walnuts. Place the chicken on a serving plate and coat with the walnut sauce. Sauté the apple gently in butter and use to garnish.

CHICKEN WITH BACON AND CAPERS
Serves 4

2 tbsp olive oil
4 skinless chicken breasts
1 onion, chopped
2 oz (50 g) smoked streaky bacon, chopped
1 tbsp flour
6 oz (175 g) chicken stock
1 tbsp tomato puree
1 tbsp capers
1 tbsp chopped fresh parsley

Heat the oil in a frying pan. Add the chicken breasts and cook, turning from time to time, for 10 minutes. Using a slotted spoon, remove the chicken from the pan and keep warm. Place the onion and bacon in the pan and cook for 4 minutes. Gradually stir in the flour. Pour in the stock and tomato puree, stirring constantly. Season. Bring to the boil and cook until it thickens, stirring. Add the capers and chicken. Cover and cook over low heat for 10 minutes until the chicken is tender. Sprinkle over the parsley and serve.

CHICKEN RAGOUT WITH CARDAMOM
Serves 4

2 tbsp olive oil
1 onion, chopped
1 lb (450 g) boneless chicken breast, cubed
8 oz (225 g) button mushrooms
8 oz (225 g) oyster mushrooms
2 garlic cloves, chopped
2 tbsp flour
4 fl oz (120 ml) milk
1 tsp cardamom seeds
salt and pepper
4 fl oz (120 ml) double cream
1 x 14 oz (400 g) can haricot beans, drained
2 tbsp chopped fresh parsley

Heat the oil in a large frying pan, add the onion and chicken and cook over low heat until well sealed. Stir in the mushrooms and garlic and cook for 3 minutes, stirring from time to time. Remove the pan from the heat, gradually stir in the flour, followed by the milk, cardamom and salt and pepper to taste. Return to the heat, bring to the boil and cook for 3 minutes, stirring constantly until the sauce has thickened. Remove from the heat, stir in the cream, haricot beans and parsley. Return to the heat, warm though gently and serve immediately.

TURKEY ESCALOPES WITH HAZELNUTS
Serves 4

1 lb (450 g) turkey fillet
2 oz (50 g) butter
4 tbsp sweet sherry
4 tbsp double cream
1 oz (25 g) hazelnuts, finely chopped
salt and pepper

Slice the turkey into thin strips. Melt the butter in a frying pan, add the turkey and cook quickly for 4-5 minutes, turning once. Remove from the pan and place on a warm serving dish. Reduce the heat and stir in the sherry, cream and hazelnuts, with salt and pepper to taste. Cook, stirring, for 1 minute. Pour over the turkey and serve immediately.

TURKEY BREASTS IN MARSALA
Serves 4

8 turkey breasts, about 4 oz (110 g) each
3 oz (75 g) butter
3½ fl oz (100 ml) dry Marsala
3½ fl oz (100 ml) milk
9 oz (250 g) ripe tomatoes
2 tbsp cream

Wash and quarter the tomatoes. Pass through a fine sieve. Melt the butter in a large frying pan and lightly brown the turkey breasts on all sides. Season to taste. Add the Marsala, milk and tomato puree. Cover the frying pan and simmer over low heat for 35 minutes, turning the turkey from time to time. Remove the turkey from the frying pan and place in a warm serving dish. Pour the cream into the pan and boil the sauce for 2 minutes until it thickens. Pour over the turkey and serve.

TURKEY SAVOURY
Serves 4

1½ oz (35 g) butter
1 onion, peeled and finely chopped
1 red pepper, cored, deseeded and diced
8 oz (225 g) button mushrooms, cleaned and sliced
1 garlic clove, peeled and finely chopped
1 lb (450 g) cooked turkey meat, diced
½ pt (300 ml) double cream
8 fl oz (240 ml) turkey or chicken stock
2 tbsp cornflour
½ oz (10 g) finely chopped parsley
1 oz (25 g) Gruyère or Cheddar cheese, grated

Preheat the oven to 350°F/180°C/Gas mk 4. Melt the butter in a flameproof casserole. Add the onion and cook, stirring, for 5 minutes. Add the pepper, mushrooms and garlic and cook for 3 minutes. Add the turkey and cook for 5 minutes, stirring occasionally. Remove the casserole from the heat and set aside. Put the cream and 6 fl oz (180 ml) of the stock in a saucepan and bring to the boil. Mix together the cornflour and remaining stock, and whisk this into the liquid in the saucepan. Simmer for 2-3 minutes, stirring constantly, until it is thick and smooth. Remove from the heat and add the parsley, and salt and pepper to taste. Stir this sauce into the casserole and sprinkle the cheese over the top. Cover and cook in the oven for 25 minutes.

TURKEY STROGANOFF
Serves 4

1 lb (450 g) turkey fillet
1 tbsp corn oil
2 oz (50 g) butter
2 tbsp brandy
1 garlic clove, skinned and crushed
salt and pepper
1 green pepper, deseeded and thinly sliced
9 oz (250 g) button mushrooms, washed and thinly sliced
4 tbsp soured cream

Thinly slice the turkey. Heat the oil and butter in a large saucepan and brown the turkey strips. Remove from the heat, add the brandy and set alight. When the flames have died away, add the crushed garlic and salt and pepper to taste. Cover the pan and simmer over low heat for 4-5 minutes until the turkey is just tender. Increase the heat, add the mushrooms and green pepper and cook for 3-4 minutes, turning occasionally. Reduce the heat, stir in the soured cream and cook for 1 minute.

TURKEY AND BROCCOLI
Serves 4

1 lb (450 g) broccoli
1½ lb (675 g) potatoes, cooked and mashed
1 oz (25 g) butter
12 oz (350 g) cooked turkey breast, sliced
1 can of condensed chicken soup
2 tbsp dry white wine
2 oz (50 g) Cheddar cheese, finely grated

Cook the broccoli in boiling salted water. In the meantime, spread the mashed potato into the centre of a warm, shallow, fireproof dish and keep warm. When the broccoli is ready, drain well and arrange around the potato in the dish. Dot with butter. Place the turkey slices on top of the potato. Warm the condensed soup in a saucepan and stir in the wine. When heated, pour over the turkey and potato, but not on the broccoli. Sprinkle the cheese on top and place under a hot grill until the cheese is golden brown.

TURKEY ITALIENNE
Serves 4-6

1 lb (450 g) cold roast turkey, cut into 1 inch (2.5 cm) chunks
8 oz (225 g) tagliatelle (dry weight)
8 oz (225 g) button mushrooms, sliced
2 oz (50 g) butter
squeeze of lemon juice
1 oz (25 g) plain flour
1 pt (600 ml) hot turkey or chicken stock
salt and freshly ground black pepper
¼ pt (150 ml) double cream
2 tbsp dry sherry
1 oz (25 g) white breadcrumbs
1 oz (25 g) grated Parmesan cheese

Preheat the oven to 375°F/190°C/Gas Mk 5. Cook the tagliatelle in boiling, salted water until al dente. Sauté the sliced mushrooms in half the butter for about 5 minutes, add a squeeze of lemon juice and set on one side. Melt the remaining butter in a saucepan and stir in the flour. Cook gently for 1 minute. Gradually add the hot stock, stirring all the time, until a smooth sauce is obtained. Simmer for about 3 minutes, season to taste and add the cream and sherry off the heat. Put the noodles in a buttered ovenproof dish. Add a little hot sauce and the mushrooms and toss together with a fork. Add the turkey chunks to the remaining sauce and pour over the noodles. Mix the breadcrumbs and grated cheese together and sprinkle over the top. Bake in a preheated oven for about 20 minutes or until the top is crisp and golden.

FISH

TUNA AND CHEESE WITH DILL
Serves 4

1½ oz (35 g) butter
1 medium-sized onion, finely chopped
10 oz (300 g) can condensed cream of mushroom soup
1 tsp dried dill
10 oz (300 g) can of tuna fish, drained and flaked
4 oz (110 g) can of sweetcorn, drained
3 oz (75 g) Gruyère cheese, grated
6 thin slices of Gruyère cheese
1½ oz (35 g) fresh breadcrumbs

Melt the butter in a frying pan over moderate heat. When the foam subsides, add the onion and cook for 5-7 minutes, stirring occasionally, until soft but not brown. Mix in the soup and dill, and season to taste. Bring the mixture to the boil. Add the tuna fish, sweetcorn and half of the grated cheese and cook for 3 minutes, stirring occasionally. Remove from the heat and place the mixture in a medium-sized baking dish. Arrange the cheese slices over the top. Mix together the remaining grated cheese and the breadcrumbs and sprinkle over the cheese slices. Place under the grill on moderate heat for 5-8 minutes until the top is brown and bubbly. Serve immediately.

GRILLED SARDINES
Serves 4

4 fresh sardines, cleaned
1 small bunch thyme
¾ tbsp sea salt
4 fl oz (120 ml) olive oil
lemon wedges
brown bread and butter

Using a sharp knife, make diagonal slashes in the sides of each fish. Break off the thyme leaves and push into the slits. Place the fish in a shallow, flameproof dish, sprinkle with salt and drizzle over the olive oil. Grill under a hot grill for about 5 minutes on each side or until the flesh is cooked. Serve with lemon wedges and thinly sliced brown bread and butter.

FISHERMAN'S PIE
Serves 4

1½ lb (675 g) potatoes, peeled and boiled
½ oz (10 g) margarine
1 tbsp milk
12 oz (350 g) plaice, filleted
8 oz (225 g) frozen mixed vegetables
4 oz (110 g) mushrooms, sliced
¼ pt (150 ml) chicken stock
1 clove garlic, peeled and crushed
1 lemon
2 level tsp cornflour
5 fl oz (150 ml) carton natural yoghurt
1 tbsp chopped parsley

Drain the potatoes and mash with the margarine and milk. Season to taste. Pipe or fork round the edge of a flameproof dish. Skin the plaice. Cut each fillet in half down the centre, season and fold in two. Sauteé the sliced mushrooms and the garlic with a little margarine for a few minutes. Add the frozen vegetables and the stock, season to taste and add the juice from half the lemon. Lay the fish on top, garnish with the remaining lemon cut in slices, cover and poach gently for about 5 minutes or until the fish is cooked. Place the potato dish under a low grill for about 5-10 minutes to brown the top. Remove the fish, drain the vegetables, reserving the juices, and place them in the centre of the serving dish with potato edging. Put the fish back on top of the vegetables. Stir the cornflour into the natural yoghurt and blend with the juices in a clean pan. Cook, stirring, for about 5 minutes, pour over the fish and sprinkle the chopped parsley on top.

SMOKED HADDOCK COCOTTES
Serves 6

8 oz (225 g) cooked smoked haddock
6 eggs
4 tbsp cream

Preheat the oven to 180°C/350°F/Gas Mk 4. Flake the haddock and mash to a fine puree, or liquidise in a food processor. Divide evenly between six individual buttered ovenproof dishes. Break an egg into each one, season with salt and pepper and spoon the cream over the top. Bake in the oven for 10 minutes.

TROUT AND ALMONDS
Serves 4

4 x 4 oz (110 g) rainbow trout, cleaned
grated rind and juice of 1 small lemon
2 oz (50 g) butter
2 oz (50 g) flaked almonds

Clean the fish thoroughly under cold running water and pat dry with kitchen paper. Season the body cavity well and sprinkle in some of the grated lemon rind. Melt half the butter in a frying pan and fry the flaked almonds until golden; drain on kitchen paper. Using the remaining butter, gently fry the trout, two at a time, for 4 minutes on each side or until the flesh is opaque. Drain on kitchen paper and keep warm while cooking the other two. Return the almonds to the pan and add the lemon juice. Cook for 1 minute, then scatter over the trout. Garnish with lemon wedges and serve with baby vegetables.

SPICY COD KEBABS
Serves 6

1 medium onion, finely chopped
6 cloves garlic, crushed
1 tbsp fresh root ginger, finely chopped
1 green chilli, deseeded and finely chopped
juice of 1 lemon
1 tbsp ground coriander
1 tbsp ground cumin
5 cardamom pods, seeds removed and ground
1 tsp ground cinnamon
salt and freshly ground black pepper
1 tsp paprika
¼ pt (150 ml) plain yoghurt
3 lb (1.3 kg) cod fillet, skinned and cut into chunks
bay leaves
lemon wedges to serve

Put all the ingredients except the last four into a blender and blend to a paste. Stir this into the yoghurt. Place the fish in a shallow dish and cover with the spicy yoghurt mixture. Leave in the refrigerator to marinate for at least 1 hour. Thread the chunks of fish onto wooden skewers with a bay leaf in between each piece. Place the skewers under a hot grill and cook for 3-4 minutes on each side, or until the fish is cooked through. Serve with lemon wedges and a few crisp green lettuce leaves.

CHEESE, ANCHOVY AND POTATO BAKE
Serves 4

1 lb (450 g) potatoes, peeled and thinly sliced
1 large onion, thinly sliced into rings
4 oz (110 g) tin anchovies
8 oz (225 g) cottage cheese
1/2 pt (300 ml) milk
salt and pepper

Preheat the oven to 375°F/190°C/Gas Mk 5. Butter an ovenproof dish and make a layer of half of the potatoes at the bottom of the dish. Cover with the onion rings and spread the anchovies evenly on top. Place the remaining potatoes on the top. Mix together the cottage cheese and milk, add salt and pepper to taste, then pour over the potatoes. Cook in the oven for 1 hour or until the potatoes are soft and browned.

KEDGEREE
Serves 4

1 chicken stock cube
8 oz (225 g) long grain rice
1/4 tsp turmeric
1/4 pt (150 ml) milk
6 oz (175 g) smoked haddock
salt and freshly ground black pepper
2 eggs, hard-boiled, shelled and chopped
1 tbsp chopped fresh parsley
2 tsp grated lemon rind
squeeze of lemon juice
3 tbsp low fat natural yoghurt
lemon wedges to serve

Bring 1 pt (600 ml) water to the boil and add the stock cube and turmeric. Pour in the rice, cover and cook for 20 minutes until the rice is tender and the liquid has been absorbed. Poach the haddock gently for about 10 minutes in the milk until the fish flakes easily. Season well. Remove from the liquid with a slotted spoon and remove all skin and bones. Flake the flesh. When the rice is completely cooked, add the chopped eggs, haddock, parsley, plenty of ground black pepper, lemon rind and juice and, at the last minute, stir in the yoghurt. Serve with lemon wedges.

NEPTUNE'S BURGERS
Serves 4

2 oz (50 g) butter
1 onion, peeled and finely chopped
15 oz (425 g) frozen cod or haddock portions, defrosted and cooked
1 lb (450 g) mashed potatoes
1 large carrot, peeled and finely grated
1 tbsp fresh parsley, chopped
1 tsp lemon juice
salt and freshly ground black pepper
2 tbsp seasoned plain flour
1 large egg, beaten
6 oz (175 g) breadcrumbs
oil for frying
lemon wedges

Sauté the onion gently until soft but not coloured. Remove all skin and bones from the fish and flake the flesh. In a large bowl mix the fish, mashed potatoes, carrot, parsley, lemon juice, salt and pepper. Stir in the softened onion and mix well. On a board dusted with seasoned flour divide the fishcake mixture into eight and flatten into round burger shapes. Dust with more seasoned flour, brush with beaten egg and roll in the breadcrumbs. Chill in the refrigerator for about half an hour. Heat the oil in a deep frying pan and gently fry the fish burgers for 5 minutes on each side, or until heated through and golden in colour. Drain on kitchen paper and serve hot with lemon wedges.

CRAB MAYONNAISE
Serves 4

6 oz (175 g) crab meat
2 hard-boiled eggs
¼ pt (150 ml) mayonnaise
anchovies
watercress

Soak the anchovies in milk until ready to use. Roughly chop the crab meat and hard-boiled eggs and mix together. Arrange in a shallow dish and pour over the mayonnaise. If the mayonnaise is too thick, mix with a little natural yoghurt. Arrange the drained anchovies in a criss-cross pattern on top and garnish with watercress. Serve with thinly sliced brown bread and butter.

MUSHROOM AND TUNA BAKE
Serves 4

7 oz (200 g) can tuna
10 oz (300 g) can condensed mushroom soup
6 oz (175 g) mushrooms, wiped
1 oz (25 g) white breadcrumbs
2 oz (50 g) butter

Slice the mushrooms, reserving three unsliced halves for decoration. Melt half the butter in a small frying pan and gently sauté the mushrooms, including the halves, for about 5 minutes. Lift out onto kitchen paper to drain until ready to add to the fish. Drain the tuna and flake the flesh. Heat the soup in a small pan, stir in the fish and simmer gently for 2-3 minutes. Add the sliced mushrooms. Butter an ovenproof baking dish and pour in the fish and mushroom mixture. Sprinkle the top with the breadcrumbs and dot with butter. Put under a medium hot grill until golden brown and crispy on top. Garnish with the three halved mushrooms.

SCALLOPS AU GRATIN
Serves 4

4 scallops
1 pt (600 ml) milk
2 oz (50 g) butter
2 oz (50 g) plain flour
2 oz (50 g) Cheddar cheese, grated
1 tbsp breadcrumbs
1 tomato
bunch watercress

Heat the milk gently in a saucepan, add the scallops and cook gently for 10 minutes. Drain, reserving the milk. Slice the tomato into four. Melt the butter, stir in the flour and cook for about 3 minutes. Gradually add the milk, stirring or whisking all the time to prevent lumps from forming. Bring to the boil and then simmer for another minute. Season well, and add half the cheese, cooking gently until the cheese has melted. Lightly butter four individual cocotte dishes and place one scallop in each. Pour over the cheese sauce, place one slice of tomato on top of each and sprinkle with breadcrumbs and the remaining grated cheese. Grill for about 5 minutes, or until the tops are golden brown and crispy. Garnish with watercress sprigs.

ROLLED PLAICE
Serves 2

4 large plaice fillets
salt and pepper
grated rind and juice of 1 lemon
1 tsp fresh parsley, chopped
4 rashers streaky bacon, rind removed
1 oz (25 g) butter
1 tbsp milk
1 small onion, peeled and grated
1 small tin tomatoes
dash Worcestershire sauce

Wipe the fillets and remove the skin. Season well. Sprinkle each fillet with lemon juice and rind, and the chopped parsley on the skinned side. Roll up, head to tail, and wrap a bacon rasher around each roll. Dot with butter, using ½ oz (10 g) only, place on a deep plate and add the milk. Steam over a saucepan of boiling water for 20 minutes. Melt the remaining butter in a small pan and sauté the onion until soft but not browned. Add the tomatoes, Worcestershire sauce and seasoning of choice - basil, mixed herbs or garlic salt. Cook rapidly for 5 minutes until the liquid is reduced slightly and the onion is soft. Carefully remove the fish rolls and grill on their sides for about 3 minutes, turning to brown the bacon. Pour the tomato mixture into a warm serving dish and put the fish rolls on top of the sauce.

HADDOCK AND COURGETTE BAKE
Serves 4

1½ lb (675 g) haddock fillet, skinned
1 oz (25 g) butter
4 courgettes, sliced
1 onion, sliced
2 tomatoes, skinned and chopped
½ tsp Tabasco sauce

Preheat the oven to 400°F/200°C/Gas Mk 6. Divide the haddock into four equal pieces and sprinkle with salt and pepper to taste. Place the butter in a frying pan over low heat and, when melted, add the courgettes and onion. Fry gently for 5 minutes until soft. Stir in the tomatoes and Tabasco sauce and cook for 3 minutes, stirring from time to time. Arrange the haddock in a casserole dish, pour over the vegetable mixture and bake in the oven for 15-20 minutes until the fish is cooked through. Serve at once.

SALMON STEAKS WITH VEGETABLES
Serves 4

2 oz (50 g) butter
12 oz (350 g) baby carrots, halved lengthwise
1 fennel bulb, cut into strips
2 small courgettes, cut into strips
1 tsp finely grated lemon rind
1 tbsp fresh parsley, chopped
4 cod steaks, each weighing 7 oz (200 g)
salt and pepper
5 fl oz (150 ml) white wine
lemon slices and parsley sprigs to garnish

Place the butter in a large frying pan over low heat and, when melted, add the carrots and fennel. Fry gently for 3 minutes, then stir in the courgettes, lemon rind and chopped parsley. Lay the salmon steaks on top of the vegetables and sprinkle with salt and pepper to taste. Pour in the wine. Cover and simmer gently for 10-12 minutes until the fish is cooked through. Do not overcook. Carefully transfer the steaks to warm serving plates and surround with the vegetables. Pour over the cooking juices and use the lemon slices and parsley sprigs to garnish.

FISH MEUNIERE
Serves 4

2 whiting or other white fish, filleted
plain flour
salt and freshly ground pepper
4 oz (110 g) butter
few lemon slices
juice of half lemon
2 tsp fresh parsley, chopped

Wipe the fish and coat with seasoned flour. Melt the butter in a frying pan and fry the fillets on both sides for about 10 minutes. Remove to a warmed serving dish and keep warm. Arrange the lemon slices around the edge of the dish and place the fish in the middle. Lightly brown the remaining butter in the pan, stir in the lemon juice and chopped parsley and pour over the fish. Serve immediately with green peas and new potatoes.

COD PARCELS
Serves 4

1 lb (450 g) frozen puff pastry
1 oz (25 g) butter
8 oz (225 g) cod fillet
salt and pepper
juice of half a lemon
1 tbsp chopped parsley
1 egg
4 tomatoes

Preheat the oven to 450°F/230°C/Gas Mk 8. Roll out the pastry thinly and cut into four 8 in (20 cm) squares. Place on a dampened baking sheet and leave in the refrigerator until required. Skin and bone the fish and cut into small pieces. Melt the butter in a frying pan and add the fish, together with the lemon juice, chopped parsley and plenty of seasoning. Mix well, cover the pan and cook for 5 minutes, shaking the pan from time to time. Beat the egg and add half to the pan. Mix well. Divide the mixture equally between the pastry squares, keeping it in the centre of the pasty. Dampen the edges of the pastry and bring each corner to the centre, pressing together to seal. Brush the parcels with the rest of the beaten egg and bake them in the top of the oven for about 15 minutes, or until they are golden brown on top. Serve hot with the tomatoes cut in half and grilled, or cold with a salad.

FISH CHARLOTTE
Serves 2

12 oz (350 g) white fish fillets
½ pt (300 ml) white sauce
1 clove garlic, crushed
8 oz (225 g) tomatoes, skinned
3 oz (75 g) fresh white breadcrumbs
salt and pepper
2 oz (50 g) butter

Preheat the oven to 425°F/220°C/Gas Mk 7. Poach the fish in a little watered-down milk until cooked. Cool, remove any skin and bones and flake the flesh. Mix with the white sauce and crushed garlic. Skin the tomatoes by immersing in boiling water for a few minutes and then peeling off the skin. Slice thickly. Put half the fish mixture in the base of a buttered pie dish, layer with half the tomato slices and then half of the fresh white breadcrumbs, seasoning well with salt and pepper. Repeat the layers and dot the top layer of breadcrumbs with butter. Bake for 20 minutes. Serve hot with a green salad.

FISH CASSEROLE
Serves 4

1 lb (450 g) leeks
2 oz (50 g) butter
1 green pepper, seeded and sliced
8 oz (225 g) tomatoes, sliced
salt and pepper
1½ lb (675 g) white fish fillets
1 tbsp lemon juice
1 tbsp fresh parsley, chopped

Preheat the oven to 350°F/180°C/Gas Mk 4. Wash the leeks thoroughly and chop into 1 in (2.5 cm) chunks. Melt the butter in a saucepan and sauté the leeks and pepper until soft and golden. Stir in the tomatoes and season well. Spoon into a greased ovenproof dish. Cut the fish into four portions and lay on top of the vegetables. Sprinkle with lemon juice and parsley and dot with the remaining butter. Cover and bake in a preheated oven for 25 minutes. Remove the cover and cook for a further 5 minutes before serving.

MALAYAN FISH
Serves 4

4 x 5 oz (150 g) haddock fillets
juice of half lemon
3 tbsp white wine vinegar
1 tbsp cornflour
2 tbsp apple juice
1 tbsp mild soy sauce
1/2 tbsp ground ginger
10 oz (300 g) can pineapple chunks with juice
half green pepper, seeded and cut in strips
1 red pepper, seeded and cut in strips
1 medium onion, chopped finely
1 tbsp dry sherry

Preheat the oven to 350°F/180°C/Gas Mk 4. Arrange the fish in a buttered, shallow, ovenproof dish and sprinkle with the lemon juice. Season to taste. Stir together the vinegar, cornflour, apple juice, soy sauce and ginger in a saucepan and continue stirring over gentle heat until thickened. Do not overcook. Add the pineapple chunks and enough juice to make a smooth sauce, but do not add too much, or the sauce will be too watery. Add the pepper, onion and sherry. Blend well and pour over the fish. Bake in a preheated oven for 30 minutes. Serve with hot cooked rice.

POACHED HALIBUT
Serves 4

4 halibut steaks (1 in/2.5 cm thick), skinned
1 pt (600 ml) milk
1 slice of onion
bouquet garni
1 bay leaf
salt and pepper
parsley sprigs to garnish

Wash the fish, pat dry and place in a large, shallow, heatproof pan. Heat the milk with the slice of onion and bouquet garni and pour over the fish. Add the bay leaf and season to taste. Cover and simmer very gently for 10-15 minutes, or until the flesh flakes. Remove from the pan carefully, place on a warm serving dish and garnish with parsley sprigs. Serve with new potatoes and a green vegetable.

DEVILLED FILLET OF SOLE
Serves 6

6 fillets of sole
5 tbsp natural yoghurt
1 tbsp Dijon mustard
1/2 tbsp horseradish sauce
1 1/2 tbsp lemon juice
chopped parsley to garnish

Wash the fish and pat dry with kitchen paper. Mix the yoghurt, mustard, horseradish sauce and lemon juice together. Place the fish in a grill pan and spread the yoghurt mixture over each fillet. Grill for 5 minutes, or until the flesh flakes. Serve immediately, sprinkled with the chopped parsley. Serve with broccoli or courgettes, new potatoes or buttered noodles.

NORMANDY COD
Serves 4

1 1/2 lb (675 g) cod fillet
2 oz (50 g) butter
1 medium onion, finely chopped
1 oz (25 g) plain flour
1/4 pt (150 ml) dry cider
2 garlic cloves, crushed
2 tbsp fresh chopped parsley
2 tbsp lemon juice
salt and pepper
flour
oil for frying

Wash the fish, pat dry with kitchen paper and cut into four pieces. Melt the butter in a frying pan and sauté the chopped onion until soft and golden. Stir in the flour and cook for 1 minute, then gradually add the cider, stirring all the time until a smooth sauce is obtained. Stir in the garlic and parsley and simmer for 5 minutes. Add the lemon juice and season to taste. Dust the fish with flour and fry in a little hot oil for 4 minutes on each side until it is just golden and the flesh is opaque. Put the fish in a single layer in a shallow ovenproof dish and pour the sauce over. Place under a hot grill for 2-3 minutes until golden and bubbling and serve at once.

BAKED SALMON FILLETS
Serves 4

4 x 5 oz (150 g) fresh salmon fillets
3 tbsp lemon juice
1 tbsp white wine
1 tsp oregano, finely chopped (or ½ tsp dried)
freshly ground pepper

Preheat the oven to 350°F/180°C/Gas Mk 4. Rinse the fish and pat dry with kitchen paper. Arrange the fillets close together in a lightly buttered, shallow baking dish. Stir together the lemon juice, white wine and oregano and pour evenly over the fish. Sprinkle with freshly ground pepper. Bake in a preheated oven for 10-15 minutes, or until the fish flakes with a fork and the flesh is opaque. When serving, pour the juices over the fish and garnish with a sprig of parsley and a lemon wedge. Serve with new potatoes and peas or broccoli.

COUNTRY FISH BAKE
Serves 4

1½ lb (675 g) white fish fillets
4 medium onions, thinly sliced
oil for frying
4 medium potatoes, peeled and boiled
salt and pepper
1 oz (25 g) Cheddar cheese, grated
1 tbsp chopped fresh parsley

Preheat the oven to 350°F/180°C/Gas Mk 4. Poach the fish, cool slightly and remove any skin and bones. Flake the flesh. Sauté the onions in a little hot oil until golden and softened. Lift out and drain on kitchen paper. Slice the cooked potatoes thinly. Butter an oven-proof dish and put a layer of potatoes on the base, then the onion slices and fish. Season to taste and continue with the layering, finishing with a layer of potatoes. Sprinkle with cheese. Bake in a preheated oven for 25 minutes until heated through and crisply golden on top. If all the ingredients are freshly cooked and still hot you can just put the dish under a hot grill to brown. Sprinkle with chopped parsley and serve.

FISH AND EGG BAKE
Serves 4

1 lb (450 g) white fish
1 medium onion, chopped
2 eggs, beaten
2 eggs
1/2 pt (300 ml) milk
3 oz (75 g) softened butter
3 oz (75 g) fresh white breadcrumbs
1 tbsp lemon juice
2 oz (50 g) Cheddar cheese, grated

Preheat the oven to 375°F/190°C/Gas Mk 5. Poach the fish until just tender, then cool. Hard-boil the eggs, leave to cool and then shell. When cold enough cut into halves. Flake the fish and place in a buttered ovenproof dish, arranging the egg halves evenly on top. Mix the onion, beaten eggs, milk, softened butter, breadcrumbs and lemon juice together and season well. Spoon over the fish and eggs and sprinkle with the cheese. Bake in a preheated oven for 40 minutes and serve with grilled tomatoes.

BACON STUFFED TROUT
Serves 4

4 trout
1 1/2 oz (35 g) butter
4 streaky bacon rashers, finely chopped
1 small onion, finely chopped
4 oz (110 g) mushrooms, finely chopped
2 oz (50 g) fresh brown breadcrumbs
2 tbsp fresh parsley, chopped
2 tsp grated lemon rind
1 egg

Preheat the oven to 375°F/190°C/Gas Mk 5. Clean and gut the fish. Sauté the onion, bacon and mushrooms in the butter until soft and golden. Remove from the heat and mix in the breadcrumbs, parsley, lemon rind and egg to bind. Season to taste. Stuff the fish with this mixture and secure with cocktail sticks. Generously butter a shallow ovenproof dish and lay the trout in a single layer. Bake in a preheated oven for 25 minutes. Serve with new boiled potatoes and a green vegetable.

FISH CAKES
Serves 4-6

1 lb (450 g) cooked fish, flaked
1 lb (450 g) cooked potatoes
4 tbsp milk
2 oz (50 g) butter, melted
1 egg yolk
1 tbsp fresh parsley, chopped
1 tsp lemon juice
salt and pepper
flour
oil for frying

Any kind of fish may be used for fish cakes, either of one variety or mixed - e.g. smoked fish and white fish, tinned salmon and white fish, etc. Put the fish in a large bowl. Mash the potatoes with the milk and butter, add to the fish and mix well. Work in the egg yolk, chopped parsley, lemon juice and plenty of seasoning. Take handfuls of the mixture and shape into flat cakes on a lightly floured board. The fish cakes can be fried as they are until golden brown each side, or they can be dipped in beaten egg and then in breadcrumbs before frying if preferred. Serve with quarters of lemon and tartare or tomato sauce.

TOMATO SURPRISE
Serves 4

4 large tomatoes
salt and pepper
4 fillets of plaice or sole
fresh breadcrumbs
butter or margarine

Preheat the oven to 375°F/190°C/Gas Mk 5. Wash the tomatoes, cut a slice from the top of each and scoop out the pulp. Place the pulp and the finely chopped tops in a buttered ovenproof dish with the bread-crumbs, plenty of salt and pepper and enough water to make a spreading consistency. Wash and skin the fish and cut into strips. Season to taste. Twist the fish strips and press them into the tomato cavities, allowing a twist to project above each tomato case. Place a small knob of butter on each tomato and stand in the prepared dish. Bake in the oven for 20 minutes.

CHEESE AND EGGS

TOMATO AND EGG SAVOURY
Serves 2

1½ lb (675 g) tomatoes
1 clove of garlic, crushed
3 tbsp olive oil
2 tsp chopped parsley
4 eggs, lightly beaten
3 tbsp grated cheese
slices of hot buttered toast

Place the tomatoes, garlic, oil and parsley in a saucepan and simmer until soft. Rub through a sieve into a bowl and add the eggs and cheese. Season, return to the pan and cook over low heat, stirring constantly, until the eggs are set. Pile onto each piece of toast and serve.

MEXICAN EGG BAKE
Serves 6

2 garlic cloves, crushed
2 onions, finely chopped
6 large tomatoes, peeled, deseeded and chopped
2 oz (50 g) can pimientos, chopped
1 green chilli, deseeded and finely chopped
1 tsp sugar
½ tsp ground coriander
12 eggs
6 oz (175 g) Cheddar cheese, grated
1 tbsp butter, cut into small pieces
¼ tsp chilli powder

Preheat the oven to 450°F/230°C/Gas Mk 8. Heat 1 tbsp oil in a large frying pan over moderate heat. Add the garlic and onions and cook, stirring, for 5 minutes. Add the tomatoes, pimientos, chilli, sugar and coriander. Season to taste. Reduce the heat and simmer for 20 minutes until the mixture is soft. Transfer the mixture to a large, ovenproof dish. Make 12 hollows in the mixture with the back of a spoon and break an egg into each one. Sprinkle the cheese over the eggs. Place a dot of butter on top of the cheese and sprinkle the chilli powder over the top. Bake in the oven for 6-8 minutes until the cheese is golden.

SOUFFLE OMELETTE
Serves 2

5 eggs, size 2
oil and butter for frying
3 tomatoes, quartered
4 oz (110 g) mushrooms, sliced
4 oz (110 g) chopped ham
3 oz (75 g) Cheddar cheese, grated
2 tbsp chopped fresh chives

Separate two of the eggs and place the whites in a bowl. Add the remaining whole eggs to the yolks, beat lightly and add salt and pepper to taste. Stiffly whisk the egg whites, then fold into the beaten eggs. Heat some oil and butter together in two small frying pans, adding the omelette mixture to one pan and the vegetables to the other. Fry the vegetables for about 3 minutes and remove from the heat. Preheat the grill. When the omelette is just beginning to set in the middle, arrange the ham, lightly fried mushrooms and tomatoes and grated cheese on top of the omelette. Remove from the heat and put the pan under the grill for a few minutes until the top is bubbling. Sprinkle with chopped chives and serve straight from the pan.

PIPERADE
Serves 4

1 red pepper, cored, seeded and sliced
1 green pepper, cored, seeded and sliced
1 large onion, sliced
2 garlic cloves, crushed
1 oz (25 g) butter and oil for frying
4 tomatoes, skinned, seeded and chopped
1/2 tsp dried thyme
1/2 tsp dried oregano
salt and freshly ground black pepper
4 large eggs, beaten

Melt the butter and oil in a frying pan and gently fry the onion, garlic and peppers until softened. Add the chopped tomatoes, herbs and salt and pepper to taste and cook for a further 5 minutes, stirring occasionally. Pour in the beaten eggs and cook gently for about 5 minutes, stirring constantly until the eggs are cooked. Transfer to a heated serving dish and serve at once.

EGGS IN NESTS
Serves 4

1 lb (450 g) potatoes, peeled
1 oz (25 g) butter
a little milk
4 eggs
salt and pepper
2 oz (50 g) cheese

Preheat the oven to 350°F/180°C/Gas Mk 4. Boil the potatoes, drain well and mash with the butter and milk, adding salt and pepper to taste. Beat until smooth. Arrange the potato mixture around the edge of four individual ovenproof dishes with a fork, drawing the fork across the top to make an attractive pattern. Break an egg into the middle of each dish and season with salt and pepper. Sprinkle the grated cheese on top and bake in the oven for 15 minutes until the eggs are set.

OATY CHEESE BURGERS
Serves 4

6 oz (175 g) Red Leicester cheese, grated
1 small green pepper, deseeded and finely chopped
1 large tomato, skinned and finely chopped
1 small onion, finely chopped
4 oz (110 g) porridge oats
2 eggs
salt and pepper
2-4 tbsp vegetable oil

Reserve 2 oz (50 g) of the cheese for topping. Mix together the remaining cheese, pepper, tomato, onion and oats in a bowl. Add the eggs and mix thoroughly until well blended. Season to taste with salt and pepper. Divide the mixture into four burger-shaped portions. Heat 2 tbsp of oil in a frying pan and gently cook the burgers until golden brown. Turn over carefully and cook until golden brown on the other side. More oil can be added to the frying pan if required. Sprinkle the reserved cheese on the burgers and cook under a hot grill until the cheese tops are golden brown and bubbly. Serve with a mixed salad or grilled tomatoes.

CHEESY POACHED EGGS
Serves 4

4 slices bread
2 oz (50 g) butter
4 oz (110 g) mature Cheddar cheese, sliced
4 eggs
4 tomatoes, quartered
watercress to garnish

Toast the bread on both sides, then butter one side. Top each slice of toast with a slice of cheese and place under a hot grill until just melting. Poach the eggs and place one on each piece of toast. Place a quarter of tomato on top and garnish with watercress.

FLUFFY EGGS
Serves 4

1 lb (450 g) sausages
4 oz (110 g) mushrooms, washed and sliced
1/2 oz (10 g) butter
6 oz (175 g) Cheddar cheese, grated
4 eggs
salt and pepper

Preheat the oven to 375°F/190°C/Gas Mk 4. Grill the sausages until they are well cooked. Melt the butter in a frying pan and fry the mushrooms. Remove the cooked sausages and slice them into pieces. Place a layer of sausage slices in the bottom of an ovenproof dish and cover with a layer of mushrooms. Using 4 oz (110 g) of the grated cheese, sprinkle some cheese over each layer. Separate the eggs, keeping each yolk whole. Place the whites in a bowl and whisk until stiff, season with salt and pepper to taste and fold in the remaining cheese. Pile on top of the sausage mixture and make four hollows in the egg white and cheese mixture. Drop an egg yolk into each hollow. Bake in the oven for 10-15 minutes until the egg white and cheese mixture is crisp and brown, and the egg yolks are set.

EGGS BAKED IN SAUSAGE
Serves 4

8 oz (225 g) sausage meat
4 eggs
1 oz (25 g) butter
2 tsp parsley, finely chopped

Preheat the oven to 350°F/180°C/Gas Mk 4. Grease four china dishes. Roll out the sausage meat and use to line the dishes. Bake in the oven for 15-20 minutes. Remove from the oven and carefully break one egg into each of the sausage dishes. Sprinkle salt and pepper on top, together with a dot of butter. Cover and return to the oven to cook for 15 minutes until the eggs are set. Serve sprinkled with parsley.

CHEESE BAKE
Serves 8

2 pt (1.1 ltr) milk
4 oz (110 g) fresh breadcrumbs
1 lb (450 g) Cheddar cheese, grated
8 eggs
1 level tsp French mustard

Preheat oven to 350°F/180°C/Gas Mk 4. Bring the milk to the boil, place the breadcrumbs in a bowl and then pour in the hot milk. Stir in the cheese. In another bowl lightly beat the eggs with the mustard, then add the milk and breadcrumb mixture. Season to taste. Butter a large shallow 5 pt (2.8 ltr) ovenproof dish and pour in the mixture. Bake in the oven for 45 minutes until it is lightly set and golden.

EGGS EN COCOTTE
Serves 4

3 rashers of lean bacon, chopped
4 eggs
butter

Preheat oven to 450°F/230°C/Gas Mk 8. Put the bacon in the base of 4 individual china dishes. Bake in the oven for about 5 minutes until the bacon is half cooked. Carefully break an egg into each dish, dot butter on each and sprinkle with salt and pepper. Return to the oven and cook for 8 minutes until the eggs have just set.

KIPPERED EGGS
Serves 4

4 pairs of kippers, heads and tails removed
4 eggs
2 tbsp milk
1 oz (25 g) butter

Lay the kippers on a foil-lined grill pan, skin side upwards. Grill under high heat until the skins begin to curl. Lower the heat and cook for 3 minutes on the other side. Beat the eggs with milk and pepper. Melt the butter in a pan, pour in the egg mixture and cook over moderate heat, stirring, for about 2 minutes, until the egg is scrambled. Place the kippers on a serving dish and spoon the eggs in the centre.

EGGS WITH TUNA MAYONNAISE
Serves 4

1 x 3½ oz (85 g) can of tuna in oil
juice of 1 lemon
¼ pt (150 ml) mayonnaise
4 eggs, hard-boiled
4 lettuce leaves
black olives to garnish

Drain the oil from the tuna and mash the fish. Stir in the lemon juice, and mayonnaise and season with black pepper. Blend the mixture in a liquidiser or rub through a sieve to make a smooth puree. Cut the eggs in half lengthwise and place yolk side down on the lettuce. Spread the tuna mayonnaise over the eggs and garnish with olives.

CHEESY CRUMPETS
Serves 4

8 crumpets
6 oz (175 g) Cheddar cheese, sliced
8 rashers of lean bacon
4 tomatoes, sliced

Warm the crumpets under a hot grill. Roll up each bacon rasher and secure with a cocktail stick. Place slices of cheese and a bacon roll on each crumpet and grill for 5 minutes until the bacon is cooked. Place a few slices of tomato on each crumpet and serve immediately.

THREE EGG OMELETTE
Serves 1

3 eggs
2 tbsp cold water
salt and freshly ground black pepper
½ oz (10 g) butter

Break the eggs into a bowl, add the cold water and salt and plenty of pepper and break up with a metal fork or whisk until they are lightly mixed. Heat the butter in a small frying pan or omelette pan, making sure that it does not brown, and, as soon as it is sizzling, pour in the egg mixture. Draw the mixture from the edges to the middle of the pan and continue to do so until the mixture starts to set and is no longer runny. Do not overcook it. Take the pan from the heat, slide the omelette straight onto a warmed plate and fold it in half. Herbs or grated cheese may be added to the egg mixture before cooking, or sautéed mushrooms or tomatoes may be placed on the omelette before folding.

BAKED EGGS
Serves 4

2 oz (50 g) unsalted butter
8 eggs
salt and pepper
¼ pt (150 ml) double cream

Preheat the oven to 350°F/180°C/Gas Mk 4. Melt the butter and pour into 8 ramekin dishes, making sure that the sides and base of each dish are lightly coated. Place the ramekins in a roasting tin and pour hot water into the tin so that the level reaches two-thirds of the way up the side of the ramekins. Break an egg in each ramekin and season with salt and pepper to taste. Pour a tablespoonful of cream over each egg and cover the roasting tin with foil. Bake in the oven for 12 minutes until the egg whites are just set and the yolks are still slightly runny. Serve at once.

CHEESE CUSTARD

½ pint (300 ml) milk
2 eggs
2 oz (50 g) cheese, grated
½ tsp mustard powder
cayenne pepper

Preheat the oven to 275°F/140°C/Gas Mk 1. Beat the eggs in a bowl. Heat the milk without boiling, and add to the eggs. In another bowl mix together the cheese and mustard, and add salt, pepper and cayenne pepper to taste. Using a sieve, strain the egg and milk mixture onto the cheese mixture. Pour into a greased 1 pint (600 ml) ovenproof dish and bake in the oven for 40 minutes.

CHEESY PUDDING
Serves 3-4

1 pint (600 ml) milk
3 oz (75 g) fresh breadcrumbs
2 eggs, separated
1 tsp made mustard
1 tbsp chopped parsley
4 oz (110 g) Cheddar cheese, grated

Preheat the oven to 400°F/200°C/Gas Mk 6. Place the breadcrumbs in a large bowl. Heat the milk in a saucepan and pour over the breadcrumbs. Leave for 15 minutes, then beat well. Stir in the egg yolks, parsley, mustard, salt and pepper to taste and 3 oz (75 g) of the cheese. Stiffly whisk the egg whites and fold in. Place the mixture in a buttered, ovenproof pie dish and sprinkle with the remaining cheese. Bake in the oven for 30 minutes until the mixture has risen.

BAKED OMELETTE
Serves 1

4 eggs
¼ pint (150 ml) single cream or very creamy milk

Preheat oven to 350°F/180°C/Gas Mk 4. Mix together the eggs and cream or milk and season well. Pour into a well buttered baking dish and bake in a preheated oven for 15 minutes until golden. Add the filling of your choice and fold over. Serve immediately.

CHEESY BAKED LOAF
Serves 4

1 small split-tin white loaf
2 oz (50g) butter, softened
2 tbsp mixed fresh herbs
salt and freshly ground black pepper
8 thick slices processed cheese
2 beef tomatoes, sliced
4 eggs, beaten
¼ pint (150 ml) fromage frais
pinch of nutmeg

Preheat oven to 400°F/200°C/Gas Mk 6. Grease a 2 lb (900 g) loaf tin. Cut the crusts off the loaf to make it fit into the tin, and slice it into about 9 thick slices. Mix the softened butter with 1 tbsp of the mixed herbs and season well with pepper. Spread on both sides of the slices of bread and arrange in the buttered tin, placing slices of the cheese and tomatoes in between each slice. Whisk together the eggs, the fromage frais and the rest of the herbs and nutmeg. Season with salt and pepper to taste. Pour over the bread in the tin and bake for 25 minutes or until the eggs have set. When cooked, leave to stand in the tin for 5 minutes to firm the loaf. Turn out of the tin onto a warmed serving dish and slice. Serve hot with a crisp green salad.

SPANISH OMELETTE
Serves 2

1 small onion, chopped
a little butter
1 tomato, peeled and sliced
2 cooked potatoes, diced
2 tbsp cooked peas
4 eggs
salt and pepper

Melt the butter in a frying pan. Add the chopped onion and fry lightly. Add the tomatoes, potatoes, peas and cook gently for 3 minutes, stirring constantly. Beat the eggs together well, adding salt and pepper to taste, then pour over the vegetables in the pan. Cook over low heat, shaking the pan occasionally, until the underside of the egg mixture is lightly and evenly browned and the top is almost set. Remove from the heat and place under a hot grill to brown the top. Serve immediately.

EGGS WITH SPINACH
Serves 4

12 oz (350 g) Béchamel sauce
1/2 tsp grated nutmeg
1 1/2 lb (675 g) cooked spinach, drained and pureed
8 poached eggs, kept warm
2 oz (50 g) Parmesan cheese, grated

Mix together a quarter of the Béchamel sauce, the spinach and nutmeg in a saucepan. Cook over moderate heat, stirring constantly, for 3-4 minutes, until the sauce is smooth. Pour the mixture into a shallow, flameproof dish and arrange the poached eggs on top. Spoon the remaining Béchamel sauce over the eggs and sprinkle on the cheese. Grill under high heat for 4 minutes until the top is brown and bubbly.

CHEESE SANDWICH PUDDING
Serves 3-4

1/2 oz (10 g) butter
4 rounds of stale cheese sandwiches
2 tomatoes, sliced
4 oz (110 g) grated Cheddar cheese
3/4 pint (450 ml) milk
2 eggs, size 2
few drops Worcestershire sauce
salt and pepper

Preheat oven to 180°C/350°F/Gas Mk 4. Cut the crusts off the sandwiches and quarter them. Butter a 2 pint (1.1 litre) ovenproof dish and place half the sandwiches on the base. Arrange the tomatoes on top, season with salt and pepper and sprinkle with half the grated cheese. Repeat with another layer of sandwiches and grated cheese. Beat the eggs and milk together, stir in the Worcestershire sauce to taste, and pour over the sandwiches. Bake in a preheated oven for 35-40 minutes, until well risen and golden brown. This recipe can be varied slightly by adding chopped, cooked bacon to the layers, or slices of onion instead of the tomatoes.

SPANISH EGGS
Serves 4

3 tbsp vegetable oil
2 medium-sized onions, sliced across and separated into rings
1 garlic clove, crushed
2 small green peppers, seeded, white pith removed and sliced
4 tomatoes, blanched, peeled and sliced
4 black olives, stoned
4 fried eggs, kept hot

Heat the oil and fry the onions, garlic and green peppers, stirring, for 5 minutes until the onions are soft but not brown. Add the tomatoes, olives, salt and pepper and cook for 5 minutes, stirring frequently. Place the mixture on a warmed serving dish and place the eggs on top.

FARMHOUSE EGGS
Serves 4

2 oz (50g) butter and a little oil
2 onions, skinned and finely sliced
1 lb (450g) tomatoes, skinned and sliced
12 oz (350 g) potatoes, peeled and sliced
1 clove garlic, skinned and crushed
2 small onions, skinned and sliced
salt and freshly ground black pepper
4 eggs
2 tbsp fresh parsley, chopped

Heat the butter and oil in a large saucepan and fry the onion and garlic gently for about 5 minutes, then add the potatoes and turn them over for another 5 minutes. Add the tomatoes and continue cooking gently for another 15-20 minutes, or until the vegetables are soft. Poach the eggs in gently simmering water for 3 minutes. Spoon the vegetables into a hot serving dish, remove the eggs from the water with a slotted spoon and arrange them on top of the vegetables. Sprinkle the chopped parsley over.

CHEESE DARIOLES
Serves 6

3 eggs
8 oz (225 g) sweetcorn
¼ pint (150 ml) milk
8 oz (225 g) grated mature Cheddar cheese
3 medium sized tomatoes, skinned, halved and deseeded

Preheat oven to 180°C/350°F/Gas Mk 4. Grease 6 dariole moulds with butter and put half a tomato in the base of each. Beat the eggs with the milk and stir in the grated cheese, sweetcorn and plenty of seasoning. Pour the mixture into the dariole moulds and bake for about 25 minutes in a preheated oven until the custard sets. Serve with a crisp green salad or fresh new vegetables.

EGG RATATOUILLE
Serves 4

2 oz (50 g) butter
2 medium onions, sliced
1 medium green pepper, deseeded, white pith removed and diced
1 small aubergine, sliced
12 oz (350 g) tomatoes, peeled and chopped
1 small garlic clove, crushed
salt and pepper
4 large eggs
1 tbsp corn oil

Heat the butter in a frying pan and add the onion. Cook over low heat until it is soft but not brown. Stir in the pepper and aubergine, cover and cook for 10 minutes over low heat without browning. Stir in the tomatoes and garlic, and add salt and pepper to taste. Heat through then place the mixture on a warm serving dish. Add oil to the frying pan and cook the eggs. When they are ready, arrange them on top of the vegetable mixture. Serve immediately.

CHEESE AND ONION PUDDING
Serves 4

1 oz (25 g) butter
2 medium-sized onions, peeled and finely sliced
1 pint (600 ml) milk
4 oz (110 g) white breadcrumbs
4 oz (110 g) Cheddar cheese, grated
salt and pepper
3 large eggs, lightly beaten

Preheat oven to 375°F/190°C/Gas Mk 5. Place the butter in a pan and heat until melted. Add the onion and cook gently until golden. Gradually pour in the milk and bring to just under boiling point. Sprinkle on the breadcrumbs and stir well. Fold in the cheese and eggs, and add salt and pepper to taste. Remove from the heat and place the mixture in a greased, shallow pie dish. Bake in the oven for 30 minutes until it has risen and is golden brown. Serve at once.

CHEESE PANCAKES
Serves 2

1/2 pint (300 ml) milk
1 egg
4 oz (110 g) flour
4 small tomatoes
4 mushrooms
1 oz (25 g) margarine
1/2 pint (300 ml) white sauce
4 oz (110 g) cheese, grated

To make the batter, place the flour in a bowl, beat in the egg and gradually add the milk. Skin, deseed and slice the tomatoes. Wash, skin and slice the mushrooms. Sauté the mushrooms and tomatoes with a little margarine in a pan, then mix with the white sauce. Cook the pancakes and fill with the savoury filling. Sprinkle over the grated cheese and place under a hot grill until they are golden.

ARNOLD BENNETT OMELETTE
Serves 2

6 oz (175g) smoked haddock fillet
4 large eggs
2 oz (50g) Gruyère cheese
1 oz (25g) butter
1/2 pint (300 ml) cheese sauce
1 oz (25g) Parmesan cheese, grated

Poach the haddock until tender. Drain, cool and remove any skin and bones. Flake the flesh. Beat the eggs until light and frothy, then stir in the haddock, cheese and seasoning to taste. Melt the butter in a 7 inch (18 cm) omelette pan and pour in the egg mixture. Cook gently, lifting the egg at the edges and moving it with a fork until it is almost set. Spoon on the warm cheese sauce and sprinkle over the grated Parmesan. Do not fold the omelette, but put under a hot grill to brown. Serve immediately.

EGGS IN ONION SAUCE
Serves 4

2 large onions, peeled and finely chopped
some lard
1/2 pt (300 ml) Béchamel sauce
4 eggs
4 rounds of buttered toast

Put the lard in a frying pan, add the onions and cook until soft but not brown. Stir in the Béchamel sauce and continue to heat gently. Poach the eggs and place on the rounds of buttered toast. Pour over the onion sauce and serve at once.

EGGS FLORENTINE
Serves 2

1 lb (450 g) spinach
butter
4 hard-boiled eggs
1/2 pint (300 ml) Béchamel sauce
2 oz (50 g) cheese, grated

Preheat the oven to 400°F/200°C/Gas Mk 6. Place the spinach in a saucepan with a little salted water and boil until it is cooked. Remove from the heat, strain off the liquid and chop the spinach finely. Place in a shallow, ovenproof dish with a little butter on top. Halve the eggs lengthwise and arrange them on top of the spinach. Gently heat the Béchamel sauce in a saucepan, stir in the grated cheese and pour over the eggs. Heat in the oven until the top is browned.

EGG AND BACON POTS
Serves 4

12 rashers of lean streaky bacon
4 eggs
3 tbsp breadcrumbs
2 oz (50 g) finely grated Cheddar cheese
1 tbsp chopped parsley

Preheat oven to 400°F/200°C/Gas Mk 6. Line four ramekins with the bacon and crack an egg into each pot. Season with salt and pepper. Place the breadcrumbs, cheese and parsley in a mixing bowl, season to taste and sprinkle the mixture over the eggs. Place the dishes on a baking sheet and cook for 10-15 minutes until the eggs are just set.

SAUCY SPICY EGGS
Serves 4

8 eggs, hard-boiled and shelled
6 oz (175 g) soft cheese
1 tbsp curry paste
4 tbsp Greek yoghurt

Halve the eggs lengthwise. Put the cheese, curry paste and yoghurt in a small saucepan and whisk until it starts to boil. Spoon onto warmed plates and place the eggs on top. Serve with freshly cooked rice.

RICE AND PASTA

NEPTUNE RISOTTO
Serves 4

1 small onion, skinned and chopped
2 oz (50 g) butter
6 oz (175 g) long-grain rice
1 level tsp dried basil
³/₄ pint (450 ml) chicken stock
8 oz (225 g) king prawns
salt and freshly ground black pepper
3 large eggs, hard-boiled and chopped
2 tbsp fresh parsley, chopped

Melt the butter in a frying pan and sauté the onions gently for about 5 minutes until soft. Add the rice and cook for several minutes, turning over from time to time, until the rice is opaque. Stir in the basil, stock and seasoning, bring to the boil, cover and simmer for 20 minutes or until the rice is beginning to soften. Add the prawns and cook for another 5 minutes, then add the chopped hard-boiled eggs and 1 tbsp of parsley. Turn into a serving dish and sprinkle the remaining parsley over the top.

CURRIED CHEESE RICE
Serves 4

1 oz (25 g) margarine
5 tomatoes, peeled and chopped
salt and pepper
1 tsp curry powder
4 oz (110 g) Cheddar cheese, grated
8 oz (225 g) cooked long-grain rice
toast triangles

Place the margarine in a saucepan and cook until melted. Add the tomatoes, curry powder and salt and pepper to taste and simmer over low heat for 10 minutes. Stir in the cheese and cooked rice, heat for a few more minutes, then pile onto a warmed serving dish. Arrange the toasted triangles around the rice.

LEEK AND BACON RISOTTO
Serves 4

1 lb (450 g) streaky bacon rashers, derinded and chopped
4 tbsp vegetable oil
4 leeks, trimmed and chopped
1 lb (450 g) long grain rice
1 x 14 oz (400 g) can tomatoes
½ tsp cayenne pepper
1 tsp lemon rind
1½ pt (900 ml) chicken stock
½ oz (10 g) butter

Fry the bacon in its own fat in a large saucepan until it is brown and
crisp. Using a slotted spoon, remove the bacon, drain on absorbent
paper and keep warm. Pour the oil into the saucepan, add the leeks
and cook over low heat for 10 minutes, stirring. Add the rice and fry
for 5 minutes, stirring constantly. Pour in the tomatoes with their
juice, add the cayenne pepper, lemon rind and stock. Season to taste.
Bring to the boil, stirring all the time. Add the bacon, lower the heat
and simmer gently for 20 minutes until the rice is cooked and all the
liquid has been absorbed. Fork in the butter and serve at once.

LIVER RISOTTO
Serves 2-3

2 oz (50 g) oil
3 oz (75 g) onion, peeled and finely chopped
6 oz (175 g) Patna rice
2 chicken stock cubes
1 pint (600 ml) hot water
1 oz (25 g) bacon, chopped
½ oz (10 g) butter
4 oz (110 g) lamb's liver
2 oz (50 g) grated Parmesan cheese

Wash the liver and steep in milk for at least ½ hour. Remove, pat dry
and cut into strips. Sauté the onion in the hot oil until soft, then add
the rice and cook, stirring, for about 3 minutes until the rice is no
longer transparent. Gradually pour in the stock, about one quarter at
a time, stirring round and frying gently until all the stock has been
absorbed. This should take about 20 minutes, by which time the rice
should be cooked. Fry the bacon until soft, then add the liver. Sauté
the liver gently until cooked through but not tough. Stir the bacon
pieces and liver into the rice. Season well and sprinkle with the cheese.

CUBANA EGG RICE
Serves 4-6

1 lb (450 g) long-grain rice
2 whole peeled cloves garlic
1 oz (25 g) butter
3 tbsp olive oil
2 peeled, sliced cloves garlic
salt and freshly ground pepper
3 oz (75 g) cooked, halved Kenya beans
½ oz (10 g) butter
1 clove garlic, crushed
2 large tomatoes, peeled and chopped
1 tsp chopped basil or ½ teaspoon dried
4-6 large fresh eggs
chopped fresh parsley

Boil the rice in 5 pints (2½ litres) water with 1 tbsp of salt and 1 oz (25 g) of butter. When the water boils, add the rice and whole garlic cloves, stir, cover and simmer for 15 minutes. Drain the rice thoroughly and rinse with cold water. Remove the garlic cloves. Heat the oil and fry the sliced garlic until it browns. Remove from the pan and fry the rice for about 5 minutes, stirring. Season to taste. Arrange on a warm serving dish. Put the cooked and halved Kenya beans in a saucepan with ½ oz (10 g) of butter and the crushed garlic and heat through. Arrange on top of the rice. Cook the chopped tomato with the basil until warmed through and arrange on top of the rice. Fry the eggs gently, sprinkle with salt and pepper and place on the rice in between the beans and tomatoes. Garnish with chopped parsley.

QUICK HADDOCK KEDGEREE
Serves 5-6

2 oz (50 g) butter
1 lb (450 g) cooked smoked haddock, flaked
6 oz (175 g) long-grain rice, cooked
3 hard-boiled eggs, 2 chopped and 1 sliced
lemon juice
5-6 slices of hot buttered toast

Melt the butter in a pan, add the flaked fish and cook gently for 3 minutes. Add the rice, chopped eggs, a good squeeze of lemon juice and season to taste. Cook for a few minutes, stirring constantly. Place the toast on individual plates, pile on the fish mixture and place the sliced egg on top. Serve at once.

RISOTTO A LA FROMAGE
Serves 4

2 oz (50 g) butter
2 onions, chopped
8 oz (225 g) long-grain or risotto rice
1 pint (600 ml) chicken stock
1½ lb (675 g) tin tomatoes
8 eggs
4 oz (110 g) grated mature Cheddar cheese
1 oz (25 g) grated Parmesan
1 bunch chives, chopped

Sauté the onions in the melted butter until soft but not coloured. Add the rice and cook briskly for 2 minutes, stirring. Add the stock, bring to the boil and simmer for 10 minutes, stirring from time to time to prevent sticking. Drain the tomatoes, chop them roughly and add them to the pan. Cook for another 10 minutes, or until the rice is soft. Soft-boil the eggs, shell them and cut in half. Keep warm. Mix half the Cheddar cheese into the risotto and check the seasoning. Place the halved eggs around the dish and sprinkle the remaining cheeses and chopped chives over the top.

SEAFOOD RISOTTO
Serves 4

2 tbsp olive oil
1 onion, chopped
1 small fennel bulb, chopped
1 garlic clove, crushed
1 small red pepper, deseeded and diced
8 oz (225 g) risotto rice
1 pint (600 ml) vegetable stock
9 oz (250 g) carton prepared mixed sea food (prawns, mussels, etc)
10 oz (300 g) Chorizo sausage, sliced
2 oz (50 g) frozen petit pois

Sauté the onion, garlic, fennel and pepper in hot oil for 5 minutes until soft. Stir in the rice, and cook over medium heat until the rice has absorbed the oil. Stir in ¼ pint (150 ml) vegetable stock. Stir over low heat until the stock has been absorbed, then add the seafood, Chorizo, peas and the remaining stock. Bring to the boil. Stir well, cover the pan and lower the heat. Cook the risotto for another 20 minutes until the rice is tender. Garnish with lemon wedges and serve hot.

PAELLA
Serves 4

8 chicken legs
4 tbsp oil
1 onion, chopped
4 tomatoes
1 tsp paprika
10 oz (300 g) Patna rice
4 king prawns
1 small packet frozen peas
pinch saffron or turmeric

Trim the chicken legs and fry in the oil until golden. Remove and keep warm. Sauté the onion until soft but not browned. Peel the tomatoes, chop the flesh, add to the frying pan and cook gently for about 1 minute. Stir in the paprika and turmeric and add 2 pints (1 litre) of water. Bring to the boil, reduce to simmering point and add the rice. Cook, turning over from time to time, for about 5 minutes, then add the chicken legs and cook for a further 8 minutes. Add the halved prawns and the peas, season well with salt and pepper and continue simmering until all the water has been absorbed. Add the saffron or turmeric, mix well and serve straight from the pan.

REGENCY RICE
Serves 4-6

3 oz (75 g) ham. chopped
2 tbsp butter
1 lb (450 g) long-grain rice
8 oz (225 g) mushrooms, sliced
8 oz (225 g) chicken livers
1 bay leaf
1 pint (600 ml) white sauce

Fry the chopped ham in 1 oz (25 g) of the butter, add the rice and fry, turning over and over, until it is opaque and beginning to colour. Season to taste, add the bay leaf and some of the stock, cooking gently until it has been absorbed. Then add a little more stock and continue in this way until all the stock has been used and the rice is tender. Turn into a ring mould and press down well, then turn out onto a warm serving dish. Gently fry the mushrooms and the chicken livers and stir into the cooked white sauce, seasoning to taste. Pour the sauce into the centre of the ring and serve.

BACON RISOTTO
Serves 4

1 lb (450 g) streaky bacon rashers, derinded and chopped
4 tbsp oil
1 large onion, peeled and chopped
1 red pepper, skinned and chopped
1 lb (450 g) long-grain rice
14 oz (400 g) can tomatoes
1¹/₂ pints (900 ml) strong chicken stock
¹/₂ oz (10 g) butter
grated Parmesan cheese to serve

Fry the bacon in a large saucepan or frying pan until crisp and brown. Remove with a slotted spoon and leave to drain on kitchen paper. Heat the oil in the pan, add the onion and fry gently for about 8 minutes until soft. Add the rice and continue frying, turning over from time to time, until all the rice is opaque - about 5 minutes. Pour in the tomatoes with their juice, add the stock, season, stir well and bring to the boil. Return the bacon to the pan and simmer gently for 15-20 minutes until the rice is cooked and all the liquid has been absorbed. Pile onto a warmed serving dish, fork in the butter and serve with grated Parmesan cheese.

MUSHROOM PILAFF
Serves 4

1 pint (600 ml) vegetable stock
2 oz (50 g) butter
8 oz (225 g) long-grain rice
12 oz (350 g) button mushrooms
1 tbsp mushroom ketchup
¹/₄ pint (150 ml) soured cream or natural yoghurt
chopped fresh parsley

Season the stock, add 1 tbsp of the butter and bring to the boil. Wash the rice, drain thoroughly and add to the stock. Cover the pan and boil rapidly for 5 minutes. Then lower the heat and simmer gently for 12 minutes. Remove from the heat and leave to stand for 30 minutes. Heat the remaining butter and cook the mushrooms on a low heat for about 10 minutes. Flavour with the mushroom ketchup, stir in the sour cream and heat through gently. Season to taste. Arrange the rice on a warm serving dish, pour the mushrooms over and sprinkle with chopped parsley.

CHICKEN PILAFF
Serves 4

1 oz (25 g) butter
4 bacon rashers, derinded and chopped
1 onion, peeled and chopped
8 oz (225 g) long-grain rice
1 pint (600 ml) chicken stock
1 bay leaf
2 oz (50 g) frozen green peas
2 oz (50 g) sweetcorn
1 oz (25 g) sultanas
12 oz (350 g) cooked chicken meat, skinned, boned and chopped
chopped parsley to garnish

Melt the butter in a large saucepan or frying pan and fry the bacon and onion gently for 5 minutes until softened. Stir in the rice and continue frying, turning the rice over, until the rice is opaque. Pour in some of the stock, season to taste and bring to the boil. Cover the pan and simmer gently until the liquid is absorbed. Pour in more stock and add the bay leaf and continue adding the stock in this way until all the stock has been used up. Add the peas, sweetcorn, sultanas and cooked chicken and cook gently, uncovered, for a further 5 minutes. Pile onto a heated serving dish and scatter chopped parsley on top.

TURKEY RISOTTO
Serves 4

8 oz (225 g) chopped turkey meat
1 oz (25 g) butter
1 onion, chopped
1 tbsp curry powder
1/2 tsp mixed herbs
pinch of garlic salt
1 lb (450 g) long-grain rice
3/4 pint (450 ml) stock
4 oz (110 g) cooked peas

Melt the butter in a saucepan, add the onion and cook until transparent. Add the meat and cook for 5 minutes until lightly browned. Stir in the curry powder, herbs and garlic, add salt and pepper to taste, and cook for 3 minutes. Add the rice, mixing well. Pour in the stock, bring to the boil, cover and cook for 35 minutes until the rice has absorbed all the liquid. Add the peas and serve at once.

SPANISH RICE
Serves 4

1 large onion, peeled and sliced
1 green pepper, deseeded and cut into strips
1 oz (25 g) butter
14 oz (400 g) tin tomatoes
2 level tsp caster sugar
1 bay leaf
6 oz (175 g) long grain rice
2 oz (50 g) grated Parmesan cheese

Preheat oven to 350°F/180°C/Gas Mk 4. Melt the butter in a saucepan over low heat and add the onion and pepper. Cover and sauté gently until the onion is soft. Stir in the tomatoes and their juices, the sugar and bay leaf. Season to taste. Cover and simmer gently for 15 minutes, stirring from time to time. Pour the rice into a saucepan of boiling salted water and simmer for about 10 minutes, until the rice is just tender. Drain well. Mix the rice into the tomato mixture in the saucepan. Turn into a buttered, ovenproof dish and cook, uncovered, in a preheated oven for 15 minutes, or until all the liquid has evaporated. Fluff the rice with a fork and sprinkle with Parmesan cheese.

TAGLIATELLE AND MUSHROOMS
Serves 4

3 tbsp olive oil
1 small onion, peeled and chopped
1 clove garlic, crushed
8 oz (225 g) mushrooms, sliced
4 oz (110 g) ham, chopped
1/2 pint (300 ml) single cream
salt and freshly ground black pepper
12 oz (350 g) tagliatelle

Heat the oil and fry the onion and garlic gently until softened. Add the mushrooms and ham and cook for a further 5 minutes. Stir in the cream, season well to taste and continue heating gently for another 5 minutes. Meanwhile cook the tagliatelle in boiling, salted water until tender, following the instructions on the packet. Drain well and mix with the cream and mushroom sauce. Pour into a warmed serving dish and serve immediately.

HAM AND NOODLES
Serves 4

6 oz (175 g) noodles
1 oz (25 g) butter
3 eggs, beaten
6 oz (175 g) thick-cut ham, chopped
salt and freshly ground black pepper
1 tbsp fresh basil (optional)
freshly grated Parmesan cheese to serve

Boil the noodles in plenty of salted water until tender, following the instructions on the packet. Drain, rinse, drain again and return to the pan. Stir in the beaten eggs and the chopped ham, season well and add the chopped basil if using. When the egg is just beginning to set, serve sprinkled with Parmesan cheese.

PENNE TUSCANY
Serves 4

1 tbsp olive oil
1 medium onion, sliced
1/2 tsp chilli powder
4 oz (110 g) smoked bacon, chopped
1 tbsp tomato puree
14 oz (400 g) can chopped tomatoes
1 tsp dried basil
salt and freshly ground black pepper
12 oz (350 g) penne (pasta quills)
grated Parmesan cheese to serve

Heat the olive oil and fry the onion until soft. Add the chopped bacon and chilli powder and cook for a further 4 minutes, stirring from time to time. Add the tomatoes, tomato puree, basil and seasoning to taste plus 1/4 pint (150 ml) water. Bring to the boil, then lower the heat and simmer for about 10 minutes. While the sauce is cooking, boil the pasta in a large pan of salted water, following the directions on the packet. Drain the pasta well, turn into a large, warm dish and pour the sauce over. Toss to mix and serve immediately with a green salad. Serve the grated Parmesan cheese separately.

SPAGHETTI WESTERN
Serves 6

4 fl oz (120 ml) olive oil
4 cloves garlic, finely chopped
1 red chilli, seeded and chopped
1 Chorizo sausage, thinly sliced
1 lb (450 g) spaghetti
2 tbsp fresh parsley, chopped
freshly ground black pepper

Fry the garlic and chilli in the hot oil for 1-2 minutes, add the Chorizo sausage and fry for 1 more minute. Cook the spaghetti in plenty of boiling, salted water until al dente. Drain well, mix with the oil, garlic, chilli and sausage and then add the chopped parsley. Season with black pepper, mix well and serve immediately.

CHICKEN TETRAZZINI
Serves 4-6

1 lb (450 g) cold cooked chicken
8 oz (225 g) tagliatelle
8 oz (225 g) button mushrooms
2 oz (50 g) butter
squeeze of lemon juice
1 oz (25 g) plain flour
1 pint (600 ml) chicken stock
salt and pepper
¼ pint (150 ml) double cream
2 tbsp dry sherry
1 oz (25 g) breadcrumbs
1 oz (25 g) grated Parmesan cheese

Cook the tagliatelle in boiling, salted water for 8 minutes, or until just tender. Meanwhile cut the chicken into bite-sized pieces and set aside. Slice and lightly fry the mushrooms in half the butter, then add the lemon juice. Melt the remaining butter in a pan over low heat, stir in the flour and cook gently for a minute. Gradually stir in the hot stock. Bring to the boil, stirring continuously, then reduce the heat and simmer for 2-3 minutes. Remove from the heat, season with salt and pepper and add the cream, sherry and chicken pieces. Drain the tagliatelle and stir in the chicken mixture. Heat through gently and then place in a greased heatproof dish. Sprinkle breadcrumbs and cheese over the top and brown under the grill. Serve with a crisp salad.

PESTO PASTA
Serves 4

12 oz (350 g) mixed plain and spinach fettucine
7 fl oz (210 ml) olive oil
3 cloves garlic, skinned and crushed
2 tbsp fresh basil, finely chopped
2¹/₂ oz (60 g) pine nuts
2 oz (50 g) Parmesan cheese, finely grated
salt and freshly ground black pepper
sprigs of basil to garnish

Boil the pasta in salted water with a dash of oil until just tender. Drain and cool. Blend the garlic, basil and pine nuts in a food processor, or pound together until smooth. Add the cheese gradually and continue blending or pounding until it is all well mixed. Season to taste. Slowly add the oil. Toss the pasta in the sauce and garnish with sprigs of fresh basil.

TAGLIATELLE VERDI WITH SALMON
Serves 4

1 oz (25 g) butter
1 small onion, peeled and finely chopped
1 clove garlic, crushed
1 tbsp tomato puree
7 fl oz (210 ml) medium white wine
salt and freshly ground black pepper
12 oz (350 g) tagliatelle verdi
5 fl oz (150 ml) single cream
8 oz (225 g) chopped smoked salmon pieces

Sauté the onion and crushed garlic in the melted butter for about 5 minutes until softened. Add the tomato puree and wine and season to taste. Simmer for about 4 minutes, or until reduced by half. Cook the pasta in plenty of boiling, salted water, following the directions on the packet. Add the cream and chopped smoked salmon to the onion mixture and simmer for 2 minutes. Drain the pasta well, return to the pan, add the sauce and mix well. Serve immediately. If preferred, this dish may be made substituting a can of red salmon for the smoked salmon.

SPAGHETTI WITH SMOKED HADDOCK
Serves 4

1 lb (450 g) smoked haddock
12 oz (350 g) spaghetti
2 oz (50 g) butter
2 tbsp fresh parsley, chopped
3 eggs, beaten
1 lemon

Poach the fish for about 15 minutes, or until the flesh is opaque and flakes easily. Drain, remove any skin and bones and flake the flesh. Keep warm. Cook the spaghetti in plenty of boiling, salted water until al dente and drain. Return to the pan and stir in the flaked fish, butter and chopped parsley and season well with black pepper. Cook gently, stirring, until well heated through, then stir in the beaten eggs until they are just beginning to set. Turn into a heated serving dish and serve with lemon quarters.

SPICY PRAWN NOODLES
Serves 4

2 tbsp vegetable oil
2 eggs, beaten
9 oz (250g) packet of thread egg noodles
2 cloves garlic, crushed
1 small bunch spring onions, chopped
1 red pepper, deseeded and chopped
1 red chilli, deseeded and thinly sliced
1 green chilli, deseeded and thinly sliced
8 oz (225g) peeled prawns
soy sauce
lemon wedges

Heat 1 tbsp of the oil in a small frying pan and tip in the beaten eggs, seasoned with a little salt and freshly ground black pepper. Fry for 1 minute on each side. Turn out onto a board and roll up. Slice the roll vertically into eight pinwheels. Put the noodles into a pan of boiling water, cover and set aside for 6 minutes off the heat. Heat the remaining 1 tbsp of oil in a wok or large frying pan. Add the spring onions and garlic and fry quickly for 1 minute, stirring all the time. Add the pepper, chillies and peeled prawns, and stir-fry for 2 minutes. Drain the noodles, add to the wok or pan and stir-fry all together for 2 minutes. Lay the omelette pinwheels on top of the mixture and garnish with lemon wedges. Hand soy sauce around separately.

LINGUINE WITH TOMATOES AND BASIL
Serves 4-6

4 large ripe tomatoes, cut into cubes
1 lb (450 g) Brie cheese, rind removed, cubed
2 oz (50 g) fresh basil leaves, shredded
3 cloves garlic, peeled and finely chopped
8 fl oz (240 ml) olive oil
2½ tsp salt
½ tsp freshly ground black pepper
1½ lb (675 g) linguine
freshly grated Parmesan cheese

Mix the tomatoes, Brie, basil, garlic, olive oil, ½ tsp salt and the pepper in a large serving bowl. Cover and leave at room temperature for at least 2 hours before using. Bring 6 quarts of water to the boil and add salt and 1 tbsp olive oil. Add the linguine and boil until tender but still firm - about 8-10 minutes. Drain the pasta well and immediately toss in the dressing. Serve at once, handing round grated Parmesan cheese separately.

MACARONI CHEESE
Serves 4

6 oz (175 g) shortcut macaroni
1½ oz (35 g) butter
4 level tbsp flour
1 pint (600 ml) milk
salt and pepper
pinch of nutmeg or ½ level tsp mustard powder
5 oz (150 g) mature Cheddar cheese, grated
2 tbsp fresh breadcrumbs

Preheat oven to 400°F/200°C/Gas Mk 6. Cook the macaroni in boiling, salted water for 10 minutes and drain well. Melt the butter in a pan, stir in the flour and cook gently for 1 minute. Remove the pan from the heat and gradually stir in the milk. Replace the pan over the heat and cook, stirring, until the sauce thickens, then remove from the heat and add the seasonings, 4 oz (110 g) cheese and the macaroni. Pour the mixture into an ovenproof dish, sprinkle with the remaining cheese and breadcrumbs and bake in the oven for 20 minutes until golden brown and bubbling.

TAGLIOLINI AND FRESH HERB SAUCE
Serves 4

1 lb (450 g) tagliolini
12 fl oz (360 ml) double cream
2 oz (50 g) unsalted butter
pinch salt
pinch grated nutmeg
pinch cayenne pepper
1 oz (25 g) grated Parmesan cheese
3 oz (75g) chopped mixed fresh herbs (basil, mint, chives, etc)

Bring plenty of salted water to the boil and add 1 tbsp olive oil. Cook the tagliolini until tender - about 6-8 minutes. Drain well and keep warm. Put the cream, butter, salt, nutmeg and cayenne in a saucepan and simmer for 15 minutes until the sauce is beginning to thicken. Whisk in the Parmesan and fresh herbs and simmer for another 5 minutes. Taste and correct seasoning. Serve at once.

SAVOURY LIVER WITH NOODLES
Serves 4

12 oz (350 g) lambs' liver
8 oz (225 g) onion, chopped
1 clove garlic, crushed
3 oz (75 g) butter
1 tbsp dry sherry
salt and pepper
12 olives, stuffed with pimientos, sliced
1 tbsp parsley, chopped
8 oz (225 g) noodles

Slice the liver into small strips, place in a bowl of boiling water and leave for 5 minutes. Drain. In a frying pan, melt 2 oz (50 g) of the butter, add the onion and garlic and sauté until soft but not brown. Stir in the liver strips and cook for 5 minutes. Add the sherry and salt and pepper to taste and simmer over low heat for 5 minutes. Add the parsley and half the stuffed olives. In the meantime, cook the noodles in salted, boiling water for about 12 minutes until tender. Drain well and stir in the remaining butter. Arrange the noodles on a serving dish and place the liver mixture on top. Add the remaining olives and serve at once.

CHEESE AND MUSHROOM NOODLES
Serves 3

1¹/₂ oz (35 g) butter
1 medium onion, chopped
4 oz (110 g) mushrooms, washed and halved
1 x 4 oz (110 g) packet of cheese slices
6 oz (175 g) noodles
salt and pepper
1 tbsp lemon juice

In a frying pan, heat the butter and cook the onion for 10 minutes until soft. Stir in the mushrooms and cook for 5 minutes. In the meantime, cut the cheese into matchsticks. Place the noodles in salted, boiling water and cook for 8 minutes until just tender. Drain off the water and stir in the onion and mushroom mixture. Add the cheese, lemon juice and salt and pepper to taste. Mix well, heat through and serve immediately.

TUNA AND MACARONI LAYER PIE
Serves 4

8 oz (225 g) cooked macaroni
salt and pepper
7 oz (200 g) can tuna
1 oz (25 g) butter
1 oz (25 g) flour
¹/₂ pint (300 ml) milk
4 oz (110 g) grated cheese
1 tbsp breadcrumbs

Preheat oven to 400°F/200°C/Gas Mk 6. Drain and flake the fish. Melt the butter, stir in the flour and cook gently for about 3 minutes. Gradually whisk in the milk and bring to the boil, then simmer for another minute, stirring from time to time. Add half the cheese and season to taste. Simmer gently until the cheese has melted. Butter a shallow ovenproof dish and layer the macaroni, tuna and sauce, adding seasoning between layers. Sprinkle with the remaining cheese and breadcrumbs. Dot with butter and bake in the centre of the oven for 15 minutes, or until it is golden brown and crispy. Serve with a crisp green salad.

PASTA BOWS WITH MUSHROOMS AND BACON
Serves 4

2 tbsp butter
1 onion, peeled and chopped
3 thick bacon rashers, diced
12 oz (350 g) shelled peas
2-3 tbsp water
8 oz (225 g) fresh mushrooms, sliced
salt and freshly ground pepper
1 lb (450 g) pasta bows (farfalle)
3 tbsp Parmesan cheese, grated

Sauté the onion until soft but not browned, add the bacon and fry gently for about 2 minutes, then add the peas and the water and cook gently for about 12 minutes. Add the mushrooms and continue to simmer, stirring from time to time. Season to taste. Cook the pasta bows in plenty of boiling, salted water until al dente. Drain. Mix the pasta bows with the mushrooms, bacon and peas, sprinkle with grated Parmesan cheese and serve.

TETRAZZINI RAMEKINS
Serves 6

3 tbsp butter
4 oz (110 g) mushrooms, sliced
8 oz (225 g) raw chicken, diced
salt and freshly ground black pepper
4 tbsp dry white wine
1 pt (600 ml) Béchamel sauce
1 lb (450 g) spaghetti
Parmesan cheese, grated

Preheat oven to 375°F/190°C/Gas Mk 5. Lightly fry the mushrooms and chicken in the melted butter, stirring from time to time. Season to taste, pour in the wine and cook until the wine has practically evaporated, still stirring. Cook the spaghetti in plenty of boiling, salted water until al dente. Drain. Stir in the chicken and mushrooms and the Béchamel sauce. Mix well. Butter six individual ramekin dishes and sprinkle the inside with the grated cheese. Divide the spaghetti mixture between the six dishes, sprinkle the top with grated cheese and dot with the remaining butter. Bake for 20 minutes in a preheated oven.

SPAGHETTI MILANESE
Serves 4

10 oz (300 g) spaghetti
1½ oz (35 g) butter
1 onion, skinned and finely chopped
1 oz (25 g) plain flour
½ pint (300 ml) water
2½ oz (60 g) can tomato puree
½ tsp dried herbs
6 oz (175 g) ham
4 oz (110 g) mushrooms

Cook the spaghetti in plenty of boiling, salted water until softened - about 8-10 minutes. Drain, stir in ½ oz butter and keep warm. Melt the remaining butter in a large pan and sauté the chopped onion until softened but not browned. Stir in the flour and cook for about 3 minutes. Gradually add the water, tomato puree and herbs and bring to the boil, stirring all the time, until the sauce has thickened. Chop the ham into thin slices, slice the mushrooms and add both to the sauce. Season to taste and cook gently for about 8 minutes. Turn the spaghetti into a large warmed dish and pour the sauce over. Toss with a fork and serve at once.

PASTA WITH HAM AND CHEESE
Serves 4

1 lb (450 g) spinach and egg tagliatelle
salt and pepper
6 oz (175 g) Parma ham, cut into wide strips
8 oz (225 g) goat's cheese, sliced
3 tbsp virgin olive oil
2 cloves garlic, crushed
3 tbsp fresh basil or marjoram, chopped

Place the tagliatelle in a saucepan of boiling, salted water and cook for 5-8 minutes until fairly soft. Drain thoroughly. Preheat the grill and line the grill pan with foil. Arrange the ham and cheese slices in the grill pan and grill for 2-3 minutes, until brown and sizzling, turning over once. Heat the olive oil in a large frying pan, add the garlic and cook gently for 1 minute. Add the cooked tagliatelle to the pan, together with the basil or marjoram. Add salt and pepper to taste and stir gently until well mixed. Arrange the tagliatelle on four warm serving plates and lay the ham and cheese on top. Serve immediately.

MACARONI WITH FRANKFURTERS
Serves 4

8 oz (225 g) short-cut macaroni
8 frankfurter sausages
7 oz (200 g) can sweetcorn, drained
¾ pint (450 ml) cheese sauce
2 spring onions, chopped
1 oz (25 g) Cheddar cheese, grated

Cook the macaroni in plenty of boiling salted water until al dente. Cook the frankfurters in boiling water according to the instructions on the can or packet. Drain them and cut into chunks. Drain the macaroni and return to the saucepan. Stir in the frankfurter pieces, the sweetcorn and the chopped onions. Stir the hot cheese sauce carefully into the macaroni and pour it into a flameproof dish. Sprinkle the grated Cheddar cheese on top and place under a hot grill until the cheese is bubbling and golden.

VEGETABLES

CHEESY SOUFFLE POTATOES
Serves 6

6 large potatoes
2 oz (50 g) butter, melted
2 oz (50 g) Lancashire cheese, crumbled
4 tbsp double cream
3 eggs, separated
2-3 tbsp chopped parsley
salt and pepper

Preheat oven to 400°F/200°C/Gas Mk 6. Wash the potatoes and prick them with a fork. Bake in the oven for 1½ hours or until tender. Cut off a lid lengthwise from each potato. Scoop the flesh into a large bowl, reserving the potato skins. Add the butter, cheese, cream, egg yolks and parsley to the potato flesh. Season to taste and mix well. Whisk the egg whites until stiff and fold into the potato mixture. Place the potato skin shells on a baking sheet and pile the potato mixture into them. Cook in the oven for 15 minutes until the mixture is well risen and golden brown. Serve at once.

SPINACH POTS
Serves 4

3 eggs
3 oz (75 g) Cheddar cheese, grated
1 x 8 oz (225 g) packet frozen spinach, defrosted and drained
3 oz (75 g) fresh breadcrumbs
salt and pepper

Preheat oven to 375°F/190°C/Gas Mk 5. Beat the eggs until frothy. Stir in the grated cheese, spinach and breadcrumbs. Season to taste with salt and pepper and divide between four greased ramekin dishes. Bake in the oven for 20-30 minutes until risen and golden brown.

CAULIFLOWER CHEESE
Serves 4

1 large cauliflower, broken into florets
salt
2 oz (50 g) butter
4 tbsp fresh breadcrumbs

Sauce:
1½ oz (35 g) butter
1½ oz (35 g) flour
1 pt (600 ml) milk, or half milk and half single cream
1 level tsp mustard
3 oz (75 g) mature Cheddar cheese
pinch of cayenne pepper
½ tsp lemon juice
salt and freshly ground black pepper

Boil the cauliflower in plenty of salted water until tender - about 10 minutes - then drain. Keep warm. Put the first four ingredients into a saucepan and whisk over a gentle heat until smooth and thickened, then add the grated cheese and cook gently for another 5 minutes. Season to taste with the cayenne pepper, lemon juice, salt and pepper. While the sauce is cooking, melt 2 oz (50 g) butter in a frying pan and fry the breadcrumbs until golden and crispy, turning over and over with a wooden spoon. Place the cauliflower in a heated serving dish and spoon the cheese sauce over. Sprinkle with the fried breadcrumbs.

POTATO AND EGG FRITTERS
Serves 4-6

12 oz (350 g) potatoes, peeled
1 small onion, peeled
2 eggs
1 oz (25 g) self-raising flour
salt and pepper
2 oz (50 g) butter
1 tbsp oil

Grate the potatoes and onion coarsely into a colander. Press out the liquid using the back of a metal spoon. Transfer the mixture to a bowl and beat in the eggs, flour and seasoning. Heat the butter and oil in a frying pan and drop spoonfuls of the mixture into the pan. Fry for 1-2 minutes on each side until crisp and golden. Drain on kitchen paper and serve immediately.

CHEESY AUBERGINES
Serves 4

2 medium aubergines, stalks removed
2 oz (50 g) ham, chopped
1 tbsp fresh parsley, chopped
1 tomato, skinned and chopped
2 oz (50 g) fresh breadcrumbs
half onion, skinned and grated
salt and pepper
6 oz (175 g) Cheddar cheese, grated
chopped fresh parsley to garnish

Preheat oven to 400°F/200°C/Gas Mk 6. Cut the aubergines in half lengthwise and scoop out the flesh. Put the aubergine shells to one side. Roughly chop the flesh. Mix the ham, parsley, tomato, breadcrumbs and onion together in a large bowl. Season with salt and pepper to taste, then mix in the aubergine flesh and 2 oz (50 g) of the cheese. Place the aubergine shells on a baking sheet and fill each one with the mixture. Sprinkle the remaining cheese on top. Cover with foil and bake in the oven for 20 minutes, then remove the foil and bake for a further 5-10 minutes until the top is crisp and golden. Serve hot garnished with chopped parsley.

CHEESE STUFFED POTATOES
Serves 3

3 large potatoes, unpeeled
1½ oz (35 g) grated cheese
salt and pepper
a little cream
a little made mustard
paprika pepper

Preheat oven to 425°F/220°C/Gas Mk 7. Wash and prick the potatoes and bake them in the oven until soft - about 1½ hours. Cut the potatoes in half lengthwise and remove most of the soft flesh, leaving just enough on the skins to retain the shape of the potato. Place the potato flesh, cream, mustard, salt, pepper and most of the cheese in a bowl and beat well. Fill the potato skins with this mixture, sprinkle on the remaining cheese and cook in the oven for 15 minutes until the tops are brown. Sprinkle a little paprika pepper on top before serving.

LEEKS IN CHEESE SAUCE
Serves 4

8 medium leeks, cleaned and trimmed
2 oz (50 g) butter
5 level tbsp flour
1 pt (600 ml) milk
4 oz (110 g) Cheddar cheese, grated
salt and pepper
8 thin slices of ham
fresh breadcrumbs

Gently boil the whole leeks in salted water for 20 minutes until soft.
Drain and keep warm. Melt three quarters of the butter in a pan, stir
in the flour and cook gently for 1 minute, stirring constantly. Remove
the pan from the heat and gradually stir in the milk. Return to the
heat, bring to the boil and continue cooking, stirring, for about 5 minutes, then add 3 oz (75 g) of the cheese and salt and pepper to taste.
Wrap each leek in a slice of ham, place in an ovenproof dish and cover
with the sauce. Sprinkle over the breadcrumbs and remaining cheese.
Dot with the remaining butter and place under a hot grill until the top
is browned.

CHEESY TOMATO BAKE
Serves 2

8 oz (225 g) tomatoes
2 oz (50 g) cheese, grated
a little grated onion
salt and pepper
cayenne pepper
1/2 tsp mustard powder
2 tbsp fresh breadcrumbs
1/2 oz (10 g) butter

Preheat oven to 375°F/190°C/Gas Mk 5. Wash, skin and slice the
tomatoes (It is easier to skin the tomatoes if they have been blanched
in boiling water for about 5 minutes). Place a layer of tomatoes in the
bottom of a greased ovenproof dish, add a little of the grated onion,
then a layer of grated cheese and seasonings. Repeat the layers in this
way until all these ingredients have been used. Sprinkle the top with
fresh breadcrumbs and dot with small pieces of the butter. Bake in the
oven for 15 minutes.

CORN SAVOURY
Serves 4

1 oz (25 g) butter
1 garlic clove, crushed
1 medium-sized onion, thinly sliced
4 slices stale white bread, crusts removed, cut into small squares
10 oz (300 g) can condensed celery soup
2 tbsp tomato puree
14 oz (400 g) can sweetcorn
15 oz (425 g) can celery hearts, drained
1 tsp paprika
1 tbsp Worcestershire sauce
6 eggs
4 tbsp milk
1/2 tsp grated nutmeg

Melt the butter over low heat in a large saucepan, then add the garlic, onion and bread. Cook, stirring occasionally, for 5 minutes until the onion is soft and the bread is crisp. Stir in the soup, tomato puree, corn, celery hearts, paprika and Worcestershire sauce. Season to taste. Reduce the heat and simmer, stirring, for 15 minutes. Beat the eggs, milk and nutmeg in a bowl, then stir into the mixture in the saucepan. Simmer over low heat for 10 minutes until the mixture is thick and creamy. Turn out onto a warmed serving dish and serve immediately.

CHEESE AND MUSHROOM BAKE
Serves 4

1 large onion, peeled and chopped
1 large green pepper, deseeded and chopped
1 oz (25 g) butter
6 oz (175 g) mushrooms, washed and sliced
4 oz (110 g) brown breadcrumbs
3 eggs, beaten
6 oz (175 g) grated Edam cheese
pinch of dried mixed herbs

Preheat oven to 350°F/180°C/Gas Mk 4. Melt the butter in a frying pan and fry the onion and pepper over low heat until soft but not browned. Stir in the mushrooms and fry for 2 minutes. Remove from the heat and stir in the breadcrumbs and the beaten eggs. Add salt and pepper to taste and mix thoroughly. Lightly grease a 2 lb (900 g) loaf tin and press in the mixture. Sprinkle the cheese and herbs on the top. Bake in the oven for 45 minutes and serve at once.

CHEESY STUFFED MUSHROOMS
Serves 4

12-14 medium-sized flat mushrooms
8 oz (225 g) small button mushrooms
4 oz (110 g) onions, chopped
5 oz (150 g) butter
6 oz (175 g) mature Cheddar cheese
1 tsp tomato puree
7 fl oz (210 ml) whipping cream
salt and pepper
1 bunch chives
2 slices dry bread, crusts removed
4 fl oz (120 ml) crème fraîche

Preheat the oven to 375°F/180°C/Gas Mk 4. Wipe all the mushrooms thoroughly. Remove the stems from the flat mushrooms, add them to the button mushrooms and chop finely. Sauté the onions in 3 oz (75 g) of the butter until soft but not coloured. Add the chopped stems and button mushrooms and cook gently for another 5 minutes. Pour into a blender or food processor and liquidise to a puree. Return to a clean pan and add half the cream, cooking gently until the liquid has evaporated. Season to taste and then put on one side to cool. Chop the chives finely and stir half into the mushroom puree together with the finely grated cheese. Spread a thick layer over the flat mushrooms. Grease an ovenproof dish with butter and arrange the mushrooms, stuffing side up, in the dish. Crumble the bread and sprinkle over. Dot with butter. Mix together the remaining cream and the crème fraîche and pour the sauce over and around the mushrooms, Cook for 20 minutes in the preheated oven. Sprinkle the remaining chives over as a garnish.

MEDITERRANEAN BEAN STEW
Serves 4

1 large onion, peeled and chopped
8 oz (225 g) smoked streaky bacon, derinded and chopped
2 tbsp vegetable oil
2 sticks celery, washed and thinly sliced
1 clove garlic, crushed
1 lb (450 g) tomatoes
2 x 15 oz (425 g) cans butter beans, drained
1/2 pint (300 ml) chicken stock
1 bay leaf
fresh basil, chopped

Sauté the onion and bacon in half the oil for about 5 minutes. Add the celery and garlic and cook for a further 4 minutes until soft. Put the tomatoes in a bowl and pour over boiling water. Leave for 5 minutes, then drain and, when cool enough to handle, peel off the skins. Cut the tomatoes into quarters and add to the bacon and onion mixture together with the beans, bay leaf and stock. Season well, cover the pan and cook for 10 minutes over a gentle heat. Sprinkle with the chopped basil and serve hot with crusty bread.

HOT BEAN RAREBIT
Serves 4

1 oz (25 g) margarine
1 onion, finely chopped
1 clove garlic, crushed
1 green pepper, cored, deseeded and chopped
1 x 14 oz (400 g) can red kidney beans, drained
1 x 15 oz (425 g) can baked beans with tomato sauce
4 tbsp tomato ketchup
1 tbsp Worcestershire sauce
2 tsp mild chilli powder
6 oz (175 g) Cheddar cheese, grated
4 slices hot buttered toast

Melt the margarine in a frying pan and add the onion, garlic and green pepper. Cook for 5 minutes. Rinse the kidney beans thoroughly in cold water, drain well and add to the pan. Stir in the baked beans with their sauce, ketchup, Worcestershire sauce and chilli powder and season to taste. Cook for 5 minutes, stirring from time to time. Add the cheese and cook for 3 minutes, stirring, until the cheese melts. Place a slice of toast on four plates and heap the bean mixture on top.

SALADS

BEEF AND POTATO SALAD
Serves 4

8 oz (225 g) cooked beef
8 oz (225 g) cooked potatoes
2 tbsp oil
1 tbsp vinegar
half a hard-boiled egg, chopped
1 tbsp spring onions, chopped
salt and pepper

Cube the beef and potatoes and place in a bowl. Mix together the oil and vinegar in another bowl. Add the egg and onions and salt and pepper to taste. Pour over the beef and potatoes.

BACON AND POTATO SALAD
Serves 4-6

12 oz (350 g) cooked bacon
8 oz (225 g) cooked new potatoes
chopped mint
chopped parsley
1 very small onion
4 tbsp mayonnaise
1 tbsp tomato sauce
dash tabasco sauce
dash lemon juice
salt and pepper
shredded lettuce
cucumber

Dice the bacon and cooked potatoes and mix with the mint and parsley. Grate the onion very finely and add to the bacon and potatoes. Mix the mayonnaise, sauces and lemon juice together, season well and add to the bacon mixture. Turn over carefully to coat. Place a base of shredded lettuce on a serving plate and pile on the salad. Garnish with curls of cucumber.

SPANISH HAM SALAD
Serves 4

8 oz (225 g) ham
1 onion
4 tomatoes
1 green pepper
2 tbsp oil
1 tbsp vinegar
1 clove garlic, crushed
salt and pepper

Cut the ham into strips and slice the onion into rings. Cut the tomatoes into quarters and the pepper into rings, discarding the seeds. Place in a large bowl. Mix together the oil and vinegar. Add the garlic and season with salt and pepper to taste. Pour over the tomatoes, pepper, ham and onion and toss well before serving.

CHICKEN AND MANGO SALAD
Serves 4

3 tbsp plain flour
1 tsp ground coriander
salt and black pepper
4 chicken breasts, skinned, boned and diagonally sliced
1 egg, beaten
3 oz (75 g) white breadcrumbs
3 tbsp sunflower oil
2 ripe mangoes, peeled and stoned
1 iceberg lettuce
2 oz (50 g) flaked almonds, toasted
juice of half lemon
2 tbsp olive oil
1/2 tsp English mustard

Mix the flour with the coriander, salt and pepper. Coat the chicken slices in this flour, then in the beaten egg and then roll in the breadcrumbs until evenly coated. Heat the oil and fry the chicken slices for 5 minutes until golden brown and cooked through. Drain on kitchen paper. Dice the flesh of one mango and puree the flesh of the other with the lemon juice, oil and mustard to make a dressing. Season well. Arrange the lettuce on the plates with the chicken slices and mango cubes. Sprinkle with almonds and serve the dressing separately.

LAMB SALAD WITH ALMONDS
Serves 6

8 oz (225 g) long-grain rice
2 sticks of celery
1 green pepper, deseeded
1 lb (450 g) cooked and diced lamb
salt and pepper
4 fl oz (120 ml) mayonnaise
half lettuce
2 oz (50 g) flaked almonds

Cook the rice in boiling, salted water for 20 minutes. Drain, wash in cold water, drain again and set aside to cool. Chop the celery and deseeded pepper and add with the lamb to the rice. Add salt and pepper to the mayonnaise and stir into the lamb and rice. Chill. Arrange lettuce leaves on a serving dish and place the lamb mixture on top. Garnish with almonds.

EASTERN CHICKEN SALAD
Serves 4

12 oz (350 g) pasta bows
2 tbsp olive oil
4 oz (110 g) mangetout
2 oz (50 g) sweetcorn
8 oz (225 g) cooked chicken, cut in strips

Mayonnaise:
1 egg yolk
juice of 1 lemon
1 tsp Dijon mustard
salt and white pepper
¼ pint (150 ml) salad oil

Boil the pasta in salted water with a dash of oil until just tender. Drain and cool. Heat the oil and stir-fry the mangetout and sweetcorn for 2 minutes over a high flame. Add to the pasta with the cooked chicken strips. Beat the egg yolk with the lemon juice and mustard until thick and creamy, and season to taste. Drip the oil in very slowly, beating all the time, until the mixture begins to thicken, then start to add the oil in a thin stream, beating all the time, until all the oil is used up. Stir the mayonnaise into the pasta and top with pepper rings.

MELON AND TONGUE SALAD
Serves 4

1 medium-sized melon
1 large grapefruit
8 oz (225 g) tongue
2 tbsp oil
1 tbsp vinegar
salt and pepper
pinch of paprika

Cut the melon in half and remove the seeds. Scoop out the flesh and place in a large bowl. Cut the grapefruit into segments and the tongue into thin strips. Place in the bowl with the melon. Mix the oil and vinegar, add salt and pepper to taste and pour over the melon, grapefruit and tongue. Toss well. Sprinkle with paprika and chill before serving.

HOT CHICKEN AND ROCKET SALAD
Serves 4

4 oz (110 g) French beans, topped and tailed
8 oz (225 g) rocket
1 small onion, thinly sliced
4-6 tbsp olive oil
3 boneless chicken breasts, sliced
2 oz (50 g) walnut halves
1 garlic cloves crushed
2 tsp grated lemon rind
juice of 1 lemon
1 tsp brown sugar
salt and pepper

Put the French beans in boiling water and cook for 2 minutes. Drain, rinse in cold water and set aside. Arrange the rocket and onion rings on four serving plates. Pour 4 tbsp of oil into a large frying pan, heat and add the chicken. Stir-fry for 4 minutes over high heat. Add the garlic and walnuts and stir-fry for 2-3 minutes, adding more oil if required, until the chicken is cooked through. Stir in the lemon rind and juice, together with the sugar, followed by the French beans. Cook for 1 minute to heat through, then add salt and pepper to taste. Divide the mixture evenly and pile on top of the rocket and onion on each serving plate. Serve immediately.

PEACH MELBA
Serves 4

4 fresh peaches
8 oz (225 g) caster sugar
1 pint (600 ml) water
8 oz (225 g) fresh raspberries
4 oz (110 g) icing sugar
vanilla ice cream
¼ pint (150 ml) double cream

Peel, halve and stone the peaches. Put the caster sugar and water in a large pan and simmer, stirring occasionally, until the sugar has dissolved. Put the peaches in a single layer in the pan and simmer gently for about 10 minutes. Remove the pan from the heat and leave the peaches to cool in the syrup. When cold lift the peaches out with a slotted spoon. Liquidise the raspberries and icing sugar together in a blender for a few seconds, then pour through a sieve into a bowl. Place a portion of ice cream into 4 decorative glasses and arrange two peach halves one each side of the ice cream. Pour over the raspberry puree. Whip the cream until it holds its shape and pipe a swirl on top of each.

BAKED ALASKA

a round or square of sponge cake
large block vanilla ice cream
frozen, canned or fresh fruit, well drained
5 egg whites
8 oz (225 g) caster sugar

Preheat the oven to 475°F/240°C/Gas Mk 9. Cut the sponge cake to the same size as the block of ice cream. Take the ice cream straight from the refrigerator and place the block onto the sponge cake on an ovenproof dish. Pile the fruit on top of the ice cream. Whisk the egg whites until they are very stiff. Fold in half the sugar and continue whisking, then fold in the remaining sugar. Pile the meringue over the fruit and ice cream until it is completely covered, making sure that there are no gaps anywhere and taking the meringue right down to the dish. Cook in the very hot preheated oven for about 3 minutes only or until the peaks of meringue are golden brown.

RASPBERRY MELON DELIGHT
Serves 6

1 honeydew melon
1 lb (450 g) raspberries
2 oz (50 g) caster sugar
½ oz (10 g) cornflour
a little caster sugar

Cut the melon lengthwise into 6 slices and remove the seeds. Bring 4 oz (110 g) raspberries to simmering point with a little water and the sugar until tender. Rub through a sieve and make the puree up to ½ pint (300 ml) with water if necessary. Mix the cornflour with a little of the puree. Put the remaining puree on to heat and stir in the cornflour mixture. Cook for 3 minutes, stirring constantly. Leave to cool. Pile the remaining raspberries on the melon slices and pour the cold raspberry puree around the base. Sprinkle with caster sugar and chill.

GALA PEARS
Serves 4

14 oz (400 g) can pear halves, drained
½ pint (300 ml) double cream
4 pieces crystallised ginger, chopped
2 oz (50 g) hazelnuts, chopped
1 jam Swiss roll

Mix together the ginger and nuts, reserving about 1 tbsp nuts for decoration. Whip the cream until it just holds its shape. Add just enough whipped cream to the mixed chopped fruit to bind it together and pile the mixture into the pear halves. Place each pear half upside down on a slice of Swiss roll and pipe the remaining cream over in a wavy pattern to coat the pear. Sprinkle a few chopped nuts over to garnish.

APRICOT FROMAGE FRAIS

6 oz (175 g) Hunza apricots or 1 tin apricots
8 oz (225 g) fromage frais

Put the dried apricots in a bowl and cover with water. Leave to soak overnight if possible. Remove the stones from the apricots and liquidise with some of the juice. Stir the apricots into the fromage frais and chill.

RATAFIA STRAWBERRIES
Serves 6

12 oz (350 g) fresh strawberries
5 oz (150 g) ratafias or baby macaroons, crumbled
3 tbsp sherry
3 tbsp orange juice
icing sugar
1/2 pint (300 ml) double cream
scant 2 tbsp milk

Place a layer of ratafias in the base of 6 decorative glasses or dishes, reserving six whole ones. Mix the sherry and orange juice together, pour over the ratafias in the dishes and leave to stand for at least 1 hour. Hull and slice the strawberries. Reserve six whole strawberries for decoration, and distribute the rest between the dishes. Spoon over icing sugar to taste. Whip the cream and milk together until it holds its shape. Pipe a swirl of cream over the top of each dish and decorate with a strawberry cut in half and a ratafia.

STRAWBERRIES ROMANOFF
Serves 6

1 lb (450 g) strawberries, hulled
4 tbsp port wine
1 1/2 level tbsp caster sugar
1 1/2 tbsp milk
8 fl oz (240 ml) double cream
vanilla sugar

Thickly slice the strawberries and put into a bowl with the port wine and sugar. Turn over with a slotted spoon and leave to soak for at least 1 hour - or longer if possible. Spoon into 6 individual glasses. Add the milk to the cream with the vanilla sugar and whip until the cream holds its shape. Spoon over the strawberries.

FRESH FRUIT SALAD
Serves 8

2 pears
2 dessert apples
2 bananas
5 tbsp lemon juice
half honeydew melon
1 mango
12 oz (350 g) grapes
1 glass of white wine (optional)

Peel, core and roughly chop the pears and apples. Peel and slice the bananas. Put the fruit in a bowl and mix with the lemon juice. Sprinkle in half of the caster sugar and place the dish in the refrigerator while preparing the remaining fruit. Scoop the seeds from the melon, remove the skin and chop the flesh. Cut the peel away from the mango and cut the flesh from the stone. Chop the flesh. Halve and deseed the grapes. Mix these three fruits in with the other fruit and stir in the remaining sugar. Pour in the glass of white wine and leave to stand for 2-3 hours in the refrigerator. Stir just before serving and serve with pouring cream handed round separately.

APRICOT CUSTARD
Serves 6

³/₄ pint (450 ml) natural yoghurt
3 egg yolks, beaten
6 oz (175 g) dried apricots, soaked overnight
soft brown sugar

Preheat the oven to 325°F/170°C/Gas Mk 3. Beat the egg yolks and yoghurt together. Chop the soaked apricots into small pieces and arrange in the base of 6 cocotte dishes. Pour over the yoghurt mixture and stand the cups in a baking tin filled with enough water to come half-way up the dishes. Bake in a preheated oven for 15-20 minutes until set. Sprinkle the top with a little soft brown sugar and place under a hot grill for a few seconds.

LEMON CHEESE FLUFF
Serves 4

6 oz (175 g) cream cheese
2 oz (50 g) caster sugar
grated rind of 1 lemon
juice of half a lemon
2 eggs, separated
¼ pint (150 ml) double cream

Beat the cream cheese and sugar together until soft and creamy. Add the egg yolks, lemon juice and half the grated rind and beat again. Whip the cream until it holds shape and fold it into the cheese mixture. Whisk the egg whites with a pinch of salt until stiff and then gently fold them into the mixture. Spoon into decorative glass dishes and sprinkle a little of the remaining grated lemon rind on top of each. Serve with langue du chat biscuits.

MANGO MAGIC
Serves 4

1 large ripe mango
1 glass white wine
juice of 1 small lemon
3 egg whites
4 oz (110 g) caster sugar
½ pint (300 ml) double cream

Peel the mango and cut the flesh away from the stone. Put the flesh into a blender and process with the wine and lemon juice until a thick puree is obtained. Whisk the egg whites until stiff and then gradually whisk in the sugar a teaspoonful at a time. Whip the cream until it just holds its shape and then fold into the puree. Lightly fold in the whisked egg whites. Pour into 4 individual glasses and leave in the refrigerator to chill for at least half an hour before serving.

MANDARIN CREAM
Serves 6

1 pkt orange jelly
½ pint (300 ml) boiling water
11 oz (325 g) can mandarin oranges
1 large can condensed milk
2 tbsp lemon juice

Dissolve the jelly in the boiling water. When completely dissolved pour in enough juice from the mandarins to make up to ¾ pt (450 ml). Leave to cool. Whisk in the condensed milk until the mixture is light and fluffy. Fold in half the mandarins, leaving the rest for decoration. Stir in the lemon juice. Pour the mixture into a decorative glass bowl and leave in the refrigerator to set. When ready to serve, garnish with the mandarins.

ORANGE POTS
Serves 6

4 eggs
1 oz (25 g) caster sugar
1 pint (600 ml) milk
grated rind of 1-2 large oranges
whipped cream
grated chocolate

Preheat the oven to 325°F/160°C/Gas Mk 3. Beat the eggs and sugar together. Heat the milk with the grated orange rind to just below boiling and gradually whisk into the egg mixture. Pour into 6 individual buttered ramekins and stand in a baking tin with warm water halfway up the sides of the dishes. Bake in a preheated oven for about 25-30 minutes until firm, then remove from the oven and leave until cool. Chill in the refrigerator. When ready to serve, top each with a swirl of whipped cream and sprinkle with a little grated chocolate.

BAKED APPLES
Serves 4

4 large cooking apples
2 oz (50 g) soft light brown sugar
2 oz (50 g) butter

Preheat the oven to 350°F/180°C/Gas mk 4. Wipe the apples, remove the cores and cut a slit around the centre of each apple with a sharp knife. Place in an ovenproof dish and fill the centres with sugar. Put a knob of butter on top and pour 2 tbsp water around the apples. Bake in a preheated oven for 35-40 minutes or until the apples are soft and puffy. Serve with the juice poured over. The centres could be filled with mixed dried fruit mixed with sugar and butter if preferred.

STRAWBERRY SYLLABUB
Serves 4

12 large strawberries
juice of 1 lemon
2 tbsp sweet sherry
2 tbsp brandy
2 oz (50 g) caster sugar
½ pt (300 ml) double cream

Line the insides of 4 glasses with slices of strawberries, pressing them firmly against the sides of the glass. Put the lemon juice, sherry, brandy and sugar into a bowl and stir well until the sugar has dissolved. Pour in the cream and whisk with an electric mixer until the mixture forms soft peaks. Spoon into the glasses and chill.

BAKED JAM ROLL
Serves 6-8

1 small packet frozen shortcrust pastry
jam

Preheat the oven to 400°F/200°C/Gas Mk 6. Defrost the pastry and roll out to an oblong shape on a floured board. Spread liberally with jam and roll up. Dampen the end and press firmly to seal. Cut in half in the centre to form two rolls. Place on a baking sheet, brush with milk and bake in a preheated oven for about 15 minutes until golden brown and cooked. Serve hot with custard or pouring cream.

TREACLE TART
Serves 6-8

1 small packet frozen shortcrust pastry
3 tbsp golden syrup
juice of half a lemon
2 tbsp fresh white breadcrumbs

Preheat the oven to 400°F/200°C/Gas Mk 6. Defrost the pastry and roll out on a lightly floured surface. Cut to fit an ovenproof plate or shallow dish. Butter the container and gently press the pastry in, patterning the edge with a fork. Prick all over. Put the golden syrup in a saucepan and gently warm for about 2 minutes, then stir in the lemon juice and breadcrumbs. Pour the mixture into the pastry and bake in a preheated oven for about 20 minutes or until the pastry edge is golden brown and the centre fairly solid. Leave to cool a little before serving. Take care when cutting as the filling can burn. Serve with pouring cream or custard.

FRUIT CRUMBLE
Serves 4

1 tin of fruit or fruit pie filling
4 oz (110 g) flour
2 oz (50 g) margarine
1 oz (25 g) caster sugar

If you prefer, instead of canned fruit you can use 1 lb (450 g) fresh fruit and 4 oz (110 g) caster sugar which have been stewed gently until the fruit is soft. Preheat the oven to 350 F/180 C/Gas Mk 4. Put the flour and margarine in a mixing bowl and rub through the fingers until the mixture resembles fine breadcrumbs. Stir in the sugar. Put the fruit and a little of the juice into a pie dish and sprinkle the flour mixture on top. Bake in a preheated oven for about 30 minutes until golden brown. Sprinkle the top with a little caster sugar. Serve hot with custard or cream, and hand round remaining juice separately if liked.

QUICK CHEESECAKES
Serves 4

8 oz (225 g) strawberries or raspberries
8 oz (225 g) full fat soft cheese
2 oz (50 g) icing sugar
4 digestive biscuits
double or whipping cream

Reserve four whole fruit and chop the remainder finely. Beat the cheese and icing sugar together and mix in the chopped fruit. Butter and base line four individual ramekin dishes and spoon the cheese and fruit mixture evenly into these. Place one digestive biscuit on top of each. Chill in the refrigerator for at least 1 hour. With a thin, sharp knife ease the cheesecakes away from the sides of the ramekins and turn them out onto individual serving plates. Carefully remove the lining and garnish each cheesecake with a swirl of whipped cream and one of the reserved whole fruits.

APPLE SNOW
Serves 8

¼ pt (150 ml) sweet cider
3 lb (1.3 kg) cooking apples (preferably Bramleys)
4 oz (110 g) caster sugar
3 egg whites
ground cinnamon

Peel, core and thinly slice the apples. Put into a heavy saucepan with the cider and bring to simmering point. Cover and cook very gently, stirring from time to time, until the fruit is soft and pulpy. Remove the lid and continue cooking, stirring frequently, until the juice has almost all disappeared and the fruit is foamy. Remove from the heat and stir in the sugar. Leave to cool slightly and then liquidise or rub through a sieve to make a thick puree. Pour into a shallow dish and leave to cool completely. Pour off any juice that may run out after standing. Whisk the egg whites until they form stiff peaks, then fold in the puree and spoon into individual serving dishes. Dust the tops with ground cinnamon.

RHUBARB AND GINGER
Serves 4-6

1¹/₂ lb (675 g) rhubarb
6 oz (175 g) sugar
8 fl oz (240 ml) water
1-2 tbsp stem ginger
2 tbsp stem ginger syrup

Wash and trim the rhubarb and cut into 1 inch (2.5 cm) pieces. Bring the sugar and water to the boil together and simmer for 5 minutes. Add the rhubarb, cover and bring slowly back to simmering point. Cook gently until the rhubarb is soft but still in pieces. Add the ginger syrup and spoon into a serving dish. Thinly slice the pieces of stem ginger and scatter over the top. Chill. Serve with whipped cream.

MARMALADE SANDWICH PUDDING
Serves 2

1 large orange, peeled and segmented
2 slices wholemeal bread, buttered
1 tbsp orange marmalade
1 egg
6 tbsp milk
demerara sugar

Preheat the oven to 350°F/180°C/Gas Mk 4. Remove all the pith and skin from the orange segments and cut each in half. Place on the base of a small ovenproof dish. Make a marmalade sandwich and cut off the crusts. Cut into fingers and lay on top of the orange segments. In a bowl beat the egg thoroughly and gradually add the milk, beating well. Pour over the sandwiches and sprinkle with demerara sugar. Bake in a preheated oven for about 30 minutes until golden and firm.

CHOCOLATE AND BANANA WHIP
Serves 4

4 oz (110 g) plain dark chocolate, broken into pieces
¼ pint (150 ml) double cream
¼ pint (150 ml) natural yoghurt
2 large ripe bananas

Melt all but 2 squares of the chocolate in a bowl set over a pan of simmering water. Remove from the heat when melted and leave to cool a little. Whisk the cream and yoghurt together until it stands in soft peaks. Mash the bananas and fold into the cream and yoghurt mixture together with the melted chocolate. Spoon into 4 individual dishes and grate the remaining chocolate over the top to decorate. Chill.

MARZIPAN APPLES
Serves 6

3 oz (75 g) ground almonds
2 oz (50 g) caster sugar
1½ tbsp water
2½ tbsp fine white breadcrumbs, dried
2½ tbsp caster sugar
6 firm cooking apples
lemon juice
1 oz (25 g) melted butter

Cream:
½ pint (300 ml) double cream, whipped
pinch caster sugar
½ tsp almond essence

Preheat the oven to 375°F/190°C/Gas Mk 5. Mix the ground almonds, sugar and water to a paste in a blender, or beat well. Set aside. Stir the breadcrumbs and sugar together until well blended and put on a shallow plate. Peel and core the apples, coat with the melted butter and roll in the sugared breadcrumbs. Arrange on a buttered baking tray and fill the core cavities with the almond paste. Bake in a preheated oven until the apples are tender - about 45 minutes. Whip the cream with the sugar and almond essence and pile on top of each apple. Serve hot.

PANCAKES
Serves 4

4 oz (110 g) plain flour
2 large eggs
7 fl oz (210 ml) milk
3 fl oz (90 ml) water
2 tbsp melted butter

Sieve the flour and a pinch of salt into a large bowl, make a well in the centre and break the eggs into it. Gradually whisk the eggs into the flour, stirring in the flour from the sides to mix thoroughly. Mix the milk and water and start to whisk this in when the mixture becomes too thick to incorporate any more flour. Keep whisking to remove any lumps. Just before cooking the pancakes, stir in the melted butter. Melt a small knob of butter in a small frying pan and when it is sizzling pour in about 2 tbsp of the pancake mixture, swirling it around the pan evenly. When the pancake is golden brown underneath, turn the pancake over and cook the top for a little while. When cooked, remove from the pan and put on a warmed plate. Cover with foil and keep warm over a pan of simmering water while you cook the rest of the pancakes. Serve with fresh lemon juice and a bowl of caster sugar.

SPICY RHUBARB SPONGE
Serves 4-6

4 oz (110 g) soft margarine
4 oz (110 g) caster sugar
2 size 3 eggs
4 oz (110 g) self-raising flour
1 level tsp baking powder
1/2 level tsp ground ginger
1/4 level tsp mixed spice
1 lb (450 g) rhubarb, washed, trimmed and chopped
2 oz (50 g) soft brown sugar
finely grated rind and juice of half an orange

Preheat the oven to 375°F/190°C/Gas Mk 5. Put the margarine, sugar and eggs in a bowl and sift in the flour, baking powder and spices. Beat for 2 minutes until smooth. Put the rhubarb in a greased 2 pt (1.1 ltr) ovenproof dish. Sprinkle with the sugar, orange rind and juice. Spread the sponge mixture over the rhubarb and bake in the centre of the oven for about 35 minutes until the sponge is golden brown and firm to the touch. Serve with cream or custard.

PINEAPPLE CREAM
Serves 6

1 lb (450 g) can crushed pineapple
1 oz (25 g) gelatine
grated rind and juice of 1 lemon
2 oz (50 g) caster sugar
4¹/₂ oz (120 g) can pineapple juice
2 egg whites
¹/₂ pint (300 ml) double cream
8 oz (225 g) can pineapple pieces

Strain the crushed pineapple, reserving the juice, and process or mash the pineapple. Measure out ¹/₄ pint (150 ml) of the strained pineapple syrup and sprinkle the gelatine over. Leave until soft and fluffy. Add the lemon rind and juice to the gelatine and stand in a pan of hot water, stirring until the gelatine dissolves. Then stir the dissolved gelatine together with the sugar into the pineapple juice, add the crushed pineapple and leave in the refrigerator until the mixture is beginning to set. Whisk the egg whites stiffly and whip the cream until thick. Fold two-thirds of the cream into the setting pineapple mixture, then lightly fold in the whisked egg whites. Pour into a serving dish and refrigerate until set. When ready to serve, pipe the remaining cream around the edge of the dish and arrange pineapple pieces on top.

ROSY KISSEL
Serves 4

1 lb (450 g) fresh young rhubarb
8 tbsp cranberry juice
2 tsp arrowroot
few drops almond essence
8 oz (225 g) fresh or frozen raspberries
2 tbsp Greek yoghurt or crème fraîche

Wash and trim the rhubarb and cut into 1 inch (2.5 cm) pieces. Put the rhubarb in a saucepan with 6 tbsp of the cranberry juice, cover the pan and simmer gently for about 5 minutes or until the fruit is just soft but still whole. Blend the arrowroot with the remaining 2 tbsp cranberry juice and a few drops of almond essence. Pour into the rhubarb and bring to the boil. Reduce the heat and then stir in the raspberries. Cook gently for about 1 minute until the juice thickens a little. Pour into a serving dish and leave to cool. Just before serving lightly swirl the yoghurt or crème fraîche through the fruit.

APPLE SLICE
Serves 4

1 lb (450 g) cooking apples
8 oz (225 g) pkt frozen puff pastry
2 oz (50 g) caster sugar
3 tbsp apricot jam

Preheat the oven to 400°F/200°C/Gas Mk 6. Peel, core and thinly slice the apples and place the slices in a bowl of cold water to which a squeeze of lemon juice has been added. Roll out the pastry on a lightly floured board to 8 inches (20 cm) square. Lift onto a dampened baking sheet and prick all over with a fork. Drain the apples and arrange attractively over the pastry to within 1 inch (2.5 cm) of the edge. Sprinkle with caster sugar and bake in a preheated oven for about 25 minutes or until the apples are soft and the pastry is golden brown. Melt the apricot jam with 1 tbsp of water in a small saucepan and use to brush over the apples. Serve warm or cold with whipped cream.

PEACH SURPRISE
Serves 6

15 1/2 oz (435 g) can peaches
1 Arctic roll
double cream
2 tbsp raspberry jam
2 tbsp water

Drain the peach halves. Cut the Arctic roll into slices. Top each slice with peach halves, core side down. Whip the cream until it holds its shape and pipe around the peaches. Melt the raspberry jam with the water in a small saucepan and sieve. Pour over the top of the Peach Surprise.

TURKISH ORANGES
Serves 4

6 large oranges
3 tbsp soft brown sugar
4 tbsp Grand Marnier or Curacao
1/2 pint (300 ml) whipped cream

Peel the oranges carefully, removing as much of the inside skin as possible. Segment the oranges, removing all the pith, and place in a large glass bowl. The oranges may be sliced if preferred, but it is more difficult to remove all the pith and skin. Sprinkle with the brown sugar and pour over the liqueur. Turn over carefully and leave to marinate in the refrigerator overnight if possible. Spoon into glass dishes and serve the whipped cream separately.

FESTIVE PEARS
Serves 4

4 William or Conference pears
3 oz (75 g) white marzipan
1 oz (25 g) sultanas
1 oz (25 g) hazelnuts
few drops almond essence
1/2 pint (300 ml) orange juice
1/4 pint (150 ml) medium white wine
2 tbsp apricot jam

Preheat the oven to 350°F/180°C/Gas Mk 4. Peel the pears and cut off 1½ inches (4 cm) from the stalk end. Scoop out the core with a teaspoon. Grate the marzipan and chop the sultanas and nuts and mix them together with 1 tbsp orange juice and a couple of drops of almond essence. Spoon this mixture into the core cavities of the pears and replace the tops. Place in a small ovenproof dish, standing them close together to prevent them from falling over during cooking. Pour over the orange juice and wine so that the fluid comes up to the filling. Add a little more wine if there is not sufficient juice. Cover with foil and cook in a preheated oven for about 25 minutes or until the pears are tender. Place on a serving dish. Pour the juice into a small saucepan and add the apricot jam. Bring to the boil and boil until the liquid is reduced a little then pour through a sieve over the pears.

LEMON PUFFS
Makes 9

8 oz (225 g) pkt puff pastry

Filling:
grated rind of 1 lemon
2 oz (50 g) caster sugar
2 tbsp double cream
1 size 3 egg
1 oz (25 g) ground almonds
2 oz (50 g) margarine, melted

Preheat the oven to 400°F/200°C/Gas Mk 6. Roll out the pastry on a lightly floured board to a 10 inch (25 cm) square. With a 3 inch (7.5 cm) plain cutter cut out 9 rounds and use these to line a 9 hole patty tin. Knead the trimmings together and roll out again. Cut into ⅛ inch (3 mm) wide strips. Beat all the filling ingredients together and divide between the patty tins, filling each pastry case about two-thirds full. Lay the pastry strips over the filling in a lattice pattern, trimming off at the edges with a sharp knife. Bake towards the top of a preheated oven for 15 minutes, or until the pastry is crisp and golden and the filling is fairly firm.

GINGER PEARS
Serves 4

4 ripe pears, peeled and cored
6 ginger nut biscuits, crushed
2 pieces stem ginger, chopped
4 tbsp stem ginger syrup
4 oz (110 g) low fat soft cheese
double cream, to garnish

Put the cheese in a bowl and beat in the crushed ginger nuts, stem ginger and 2 tbsp of the syrup. Spoon this mixture into the core cavities of the pears and sandwich them back together again. Place in individual serving dishes and drizzle the remaining syrup over the top. Chill. Just before serving pipe a swirl of whipped cream on top of each of the pears.

APPLE TART
Serves 8

Pastry:
3 oz (75 g) butter
5 oz (150 g) plain flour
1 tbsp caster sugar
1 egg yolk
1-2 tbsp water

Filling:
1 lb (450 g) cooking apples
1 oz (25 g) granulated sugar
4 red-skinned dessert apples
2 oz (50 g) caster sugar

Preheat the oven to 375°F/190°C/Gas Mk 5. Make the pastry in the usual way by rubbing the butter into the flour until it resembles fine breadcrumbs, stir in the sugar and bind together with the egg yolk and enough water to make a pliable but not sticky dough. Knead lightly until smooth, then roll out on a very lightly floured board and use to line a fluted flan tin. Press the pastry down well, prick all over and trim. Line with greaseproof paper and baking beans and cook blind in a preheated oven for about 20 minutes. Remove the beans and paper and return to the oven for another 5 minutes. Cool. Peel, core and chop the apples. Cook the apples gently over low heat with the granulated sugar until they are pulpy. Cool them a little and puree in a blender or by pressing through a sieve. Fill the centre of the pastry case with the apple puree. Core and slice the dessert apples and lay over the puree. When covered sprinkle with the caster sugar and put under a hot grill until browned all over, watching to make sure the sugar does not burn. Serve cold with cream.

CAKES & BISCUITS

APPLE SCONES
Makes 10

8 oz (225 g) self-raising flour
1 tsp baking powder
2 oz (50 g) butter
1 tbsp caster sugar
1 oz (25 g) raisins
1 dessert apple, peeled, cored and diced
3-4 fl oz (90-120 ml) milk
1 tbsp demerara sugar
1 tsp sesame seeds

Preheat the oven to 425°F/220°C/Gas Mk 7. Sieve the flour and baking powder together and rub in the butter until the mixture resembles fine breadcrumbs. Stir in the caster sugar, raisins and apple and mix to a soft dough with as much milk as is required. Roll out thickly on a lightly floured surface and cut into rounds with a plain cutter. Brush the tops with a little milk. Mix the demerara sugar and sesame seeds together and sprinkle on top. Bake in a preheated oven for 10-12 minutes until well risen and golden.

COCONUT MACAROONS
Makes 10

8 oz (225 g) soft light brown sugar
6 oz (175 g) desiccated coconut
2 egg whites
rice paper

Preheat the oven to 300°F/150°C/Gas Mk 2. Beat the egg whites until stiff and then beat in half the sugar until peaks form. Fold in the remaining sugar and then fold the coconut in very gently. Spoon some of the mixture onto the rice paper making oval shapes. Bake in a preheated oven for about 35 minutes until golden brown.

CINNAMON SHORTBREADS
Makes 20

4 oz (110 g) unsalted butter
2 oz (50 g) caster sugar
4 oz (110 g) plain flour
2 oz (50 g) ground rice
1¹/₂ tsp ground cinnamon
caster sugar for dusting

Preheat the oven to 350°F/180°C/Gas Mk 4. Cream the butter and sugar together until very light and fluffy. Sift the flour with the ground rice and cinnamon and gradually work into the creamed ingredients. Turn out onto a floured surface and pat or roll to a thickness of ¹/₄ inch (6 mm). Cut into diamond shapes with shaped cutters if available, or with a sharp knife, and place on a greased baking tray. Prick with a fork and bake in a preheated oven for 15-20 minutes or until the shortbreads are pale golden. They will still be soft at this stage but will become crisp when they are cool. Dust with caster sugar and cool on a wire rack. Eat within 5 days.

APPLE AND DATE FLAPJACKS
Makes 10

6 oz (175 g) butter
6 oz (175 g) soft light brown sugar
3 oz (75 g) golden syrup
12 oz (350 g) rolled oats
8 oz (225 g) cooking apples, peeled, cored and sliced
8 oz (225 g) chopped dates
grated rind of 1 orange and a little juice

Preheat the oven to 350°F/180°C/Gas Mk 4. Melt the butter, sugar and golden syrup in a saucepan and stir in the rolled oats. Spoon two-thirds of this mixture into a greased 7 inch (17.5 cm) square tin. Cook in a preheated oven for 20 minutes. Cook the apples with the chopped dates, a squeeze of orange juice and the grated rind of the orange until thick and pulpy. Spoon onto the flapjack base, sprinkle with the remaining oat mixture and bake for a further 30 minutes. Serve cold, cut into slices.

TROPICAL ROCK CAKES
Makes 12

12 oz (350 g) plain flour
3 tsp baking powder
1 tsp mixed spice
6 oz (175 g) butter, diced
2 oz (50 g) desiccated coconut
3 oz (75 g) dried pineapple pieces
3 oz (75 g) dried papaya pieces
3 oz (75 g) demerara sugar
2 eggs, size 3, beaten
3 tbsp milk

Preheat the oven to 400°F/200°C/Gas Mk 6. Sieve the flour, baking powder and mixed spice together into a mixing bowl. Add the butter and rub into the dry ingredients until the mixture resembles fine breadcrumbs. Stir in the coconut, fruit and sugar. Make a well in the centre and stir in the eggs and milk beaten together. Bind loosely with a fork until a stiff but crumbly mixture is obtained. Using two forks, shape into rough heaps on two lightly greased baking sheets and bake in a preheated oven for 20 minutes until golden. Cool on a wire rack.

PEACH AND RASPBERRY STREUSEL
Serves 10

6 oz (175 g) butter, softened
2 oz (50 g) caster sugar
12 oz (350 g) plain flour
1 egg, beaten
1 tsp baking powder
5 ripe peaches, halved, skinned and stoned (drained, canned peach slices may be used if fresh ones aren't available)
4 oz (110 g) fresh raspberries

Preheat the oven to 375°F/190°C/Gas Mk 5. Cream the butter and sugar together until light and fluffy, then lightly stir in the flour until the mixture resembles fine breadcrumbs. Set aside 7 oz (200 g) of the mixture for the topping. Add the beaten egg and baking powder to the remaining mixture and mix thoroughly to make a soft dough. Press into the base of a lightly oiled 11 x 7 inch (28 x 18 cm) baking tin. Arrange the sliced peaches and the raspberries over the base and spoon the crumble mixture over the top. Bake in a preheated oven for 30-35 minutes until the crumble is becomes golden in colour. Leave to cool before cutting.

QUICK CHOCOLATE CAKE
Serves 8

4 oz (110 g) margarine
3 oz (75 g) soft dark brown sugar
3 oz (75 g) wholemeal self-raising flour
1 tbsp cocoa
2 eggs
4 oz (110 g) plain chocolate

Preheat the oven to 350°F/180°C/Gas Mk 4. Put all the ingredients together in a bowl and beat until smooth. Spoon into a greased and lined 7 inch (18 cm) round cake tin and bake in a preheated oven for 25-30 minutes, or until the centre is cooked when tested with a skewer. Leave to cool for 5 minutes, then turn onto a wire rack. Melt the chocolate in a bowl over a pan of simmering water, spread over the cake and swirl. Leave to cool. This is best eaten on the same day.

SPANISH CHURROS
Serves 4-6

3 oz (75 g) butter
7¹/₂ fl oz (220 ml) water
4 oz (110 g) plain flour
1¹/₂ oz (35g) plus ¹/₄ tsp caster sugar
3 eggs, size 3
oil for deep-frying

Put the butter and water in a heavy-based saucepan and cook over a low heat until the butter has melted. Sift the flour and ¹/₄ tsp caster sugar onto a large square of greaseproof paper folded down the centre. Bring the butter and water to a rolling boil, shoot in the flour from the greaseproof paper, take off the heat and beat vigorously. Leave to cool slightly. Heat the oil for frying to 375°F/190°C. Lightly beat the eggs and gradually beat into the butter and flour paste until smooth and glossy. Spoon into a piping bag fitted with a ¹/₂ inch (1.25 cm) star nozzle. Pipe four or five 4 inch (10 cm) lengths at a time into the hot oil, cutting the paste off with kitchen scissors. Fry for 2 minutes until golden. Remove with a slotted spoon and drain on kitchen paper. When cold, dredge heavily with caster sugar. A little ground cinnamon may be mixed with the caster sugar when dredging.

APRICOT AND OAT CRUNCHIES
Makes 10

3 oz (75 g) butter
1 oz (25 g) soft light brown sugar
1 level tbsp golden syrup
1 level tbsp cocoa powder
6 oz (175 g) crunchy oat cereal
1 oz (25 g) flaked almonds
1 oz (25 g) dried apricots, chopped

Melt the butter in a saucepan with the sugar, golden syrup and cocoa. Mix together the roasted oat cereal, almonds and chopped apricots and fold in the liquid mixture. Spoon the mixture into a greased and lined 7 inch (18 cm) square tin. Level the top, chill and cut into fingers.

COCONUT FINGERS
Makes 16 fingers

6 oz (175 g) plain flour
3 oz (75 g) margarine
2 oz (50 g) caster sugar
2 eggs, size 2, separated
½ tsp almond essence
4 tbsp jam

Topping:
4 oz (110 g) caster sugar
1 level tbsp self-raising flour
3 oz (75 g) desiccated coconut

Preheat the oven to 350°F/180°C/Gas Mk 4. Rub the margarine into the flour until it resembles fine breadcrumbs. Stir in the sugar, egg yolks and almond essence until the ingredients bind together. Put onto a lightly floured board and knead lightly until smooth. Roll out to fit the base of a shallow 7 x 11 inch (18 x 28 cm) baking tin, and spread with jam. Whisk the egg whites until stiff, then lightly fold in the sugar, flour and coconut using a metal spoon. Spread the meringue mixture over the jam and bake in a preheated oven for 30 minutes until golden. Allow to cool for 5 minutes before cutting into fingers, then leave to cool completely before removing from the tin.

CURD TART
Serves 6-8

8 oz (225 g) pkt ready-made shortcrust pastry

Filling:
8 oz (225 g) cream cheese
2 size 3 eggs, separated
2 oz (50 g) caster sugar
grated rind of 1 lemon
2 oz (50 g) currants
pinch nutmeg

Preheat the oven to 400°F/200°C/Gas Mk 6. Roll out the pastry on a lightly floured board and use to line an 8 inch (20 cm) flan tin. Prick the pastry base with a fork. Beat together the cream cheese, egg yolks, sugar and lemon rind. Whisk the egg whites until stiff and fold into the cream cheese mixture with the currants. Spoon into the pastry case and sprinkle with nutmeg. Bake in the centre of the oven for 20 minutes, then reduce the temperature to 350°F/180°C/Gas Mk 4 and cook for a further 15 minutes or until the filling is firm to the touch. Cool before serving.

CINNAMON DROP SCONES
Makes 24

8 oz (225 g) self-raising flour
1 tsp ground cinnamon
1/2 tsp bicarbonate of soda
1 tsp cream of tartar
2 tbsp caster sugar
1 egg
1/2 pint (300 ml) milk
4 tbsp oil

Sift the flour, cinnamon, bicarbonate of soda and cream of tartar into a bowl. Stir in the sugar. Add the egg and a little milk and whisk until smooth. Gradually whisk in the remaining milk and mix well. Heat the oil in a large, heavy-based frying pan. Drop tablespoonfuls of the mixture into the pan, spaced well apart, and cook for 1-2 minutes until bubbles appear on the surface and the underside is golden. Turn the scones over and cook until golden. Remove from the pan and keep warm. Repeat with the remaining mixture, oiling the pan between batches. Serve hot, spread with butter and honey.

CHOC AND NUT SQUARES
Makes 15

4 oz (110 g) butter
1 oz (25 g) cocoa
2 eggs
8 oz (225 g) caster sugar
1 tsp vanilla essence
2 oz (50 g) self-raising flour
4 oz (110 g) mixed chopped nuts
2 oz (50 g) raisins
3 tbsp honey
¼ tsp ground cinnamon
2 tbsp demerara sugar

Preheat the oven to 350°F/180°C/Gas Mk 4. Melt the butter in a small saucepan and mix in the cocoa. Leave to cool. Whisk the eggs, sugar and vanilla essence together until thick and fluffy and a trail remains on the surface when you remove the beater. Fold the sifted flour, nuts and raisins gently into the egg mixture, followed by the cocoa mixture. Grease and line the base and sides of a 11 x 7 inch (28 x 18 cm) rectangular tin and spoon the mixture in. Level the top and bake in a preheated oven until well risen and firm to the touch. Heat the honey and cinnamon in a small pan, prick the cake surface and spoon the honey mixture over. Leave to cool in the tin. Turn the cake out, remove the paper and sprinkle with demerara sugar. Cut into squares.

APRICOT REFRIGERATOR CAKE
Makes 8

4 oz (110 g) dried apricots
2 oz (50 g) seedless raisins
4 oz (110 g) butter
3 oz (75 g) golden syrup
1 oz (25 g) cocoa powder
12 oz (350 g) digestive biscuits, crumbled

Soak the apricots and raisins separately overnight in cold water. Drain well. Put the butter, golden syrup and cocoa powder into a saucepan and stir over gentle heat until smooth and blended. Roughly chop the apricots and stir into the cocoa mixture together with the raisins and biscuit crumbs. Spoon into a base-lined 8 inch (20 cm) non-stick, round cake tin. Refrigerate overnight. Remove from the tin, peel off the base paper and cut into thin wedges.

MARBLED MALLOW CAKES
Makes 18-20

14 oz (400 g) can condensed milk
8 oz (225 g) caster sugar
4 oz (110 g) plain flour
1 oz (25 g) cocoa
4 oz (110 g) butter
3 oz (75 g) walnuts, chopped
5 oz (150 g) roughly crushed sweetmeal biscuits
1 tsp vanilla essence
6 oz (175 g) marshmallows, chopped
6 oz (175 g) plain chocolate

Put the condensed milk, caster sugar, plain flour, cocoa and butter in a pan. Stir together, slowly bring to the boil, still stirring, and cook for 1 minute. Cool slightly and then stir in the walnuts, biscuits and vanilla essence. Add the marshmallows and stir lightly to achieve a marbled appearance. Pour into a greased 9 x 12 inch (23 x 30 cm) tin and leave overnight to set. Turn out and cut into shapes with a cutter. Melt the chocolate in a small basin set over hot water and dip half of each cake into the chocolate. Leave until the chocolate sets.

CARAMEL WALNUT CRUNCHIES
Makes 25

6 oz (175 g) flour
8 oz (225 g) soft brown sugar
3 oz (75 g) softened butter
2 oz (50 g) chopped walnuts
4 oz (110 g) butter
6 oz (175 g) milk chocolate drops

Preheat oven to 350°F/180°C/Gas Mk 4. Mix the flour, 6 oz (175 g) of the soft brown sugar and the softened butter together until soft and crumbly. Press into the base of an ungreased 9 in (23 cm) square baking tin. Sprinkle the chopped walnuts over the top. In a small saucepan bring 4 oz (110 g) butter and the remaining sugar to the boil. Simmer for 1 minute, stirring. Remove from the heat and pour over the walnuts, covering all the pastry. Bake in a preheated oven for 20 minutes until the caramel is bubbling over the entire surface. Remove from the oven and sprinkle with the chocolate drops. Leave until the chocolate has melted and then gently swirl a knife through the caramel to create a marbled effect. Cool in the tin before cutting.

FLORENTINES
Makes 18

2 oz (50 g) margarine
2 oz (50 g) caster sugar
2 tsp milk
1 tbsp plain flour
2 oz (50 g) mixed nuts, finely chopped
3 glacé cherries, chopped
2 tbsp chopped mixed peel
1 tbsp sultanas, chopped
4 oz (110 g) plain chocolate

Preheat oven to 350°F/180°C/Gas Mk 4. Melt the margarine in a pan and stir in the sugar. Bring slowly to the boil, stirring occasionally. Remove from the heat and stir in the milk, flour, nuts, cherries, peel and sultanas. Cool slightly. Grease and line two baking sheets and put teaspoonfuls of the mixture, spaced well apart, on the paper. Bake, one sheet at a time, in the oven for 8-10 minutes until golden. Remove with an oiled palette knife and cool on a wire rack. Cook the remaining mixture in the same way. Break the chocolate into a small bowl and melt over hot water. Spread the melted chocolate on to the flat side of the Florentines and mark a pattern with a fork. Leave to cool.

BRANDY SNAPS
Makes 8

2 oz (50 g) butter
2 oz (50 g) demerara sugar
2 oz (50 g) golden syrup
2 oz (50 g) plain flour
1/2 tsp ground ginger
5 fl oz (150 ml) double cream, whipped
grated rind and juice of half a lemon

Preheat oven to 350°F/180°C/Gas Mk 4. Melt the butter in a pan, add the sugar and syrup and heat gently until the sugar dissolves. Remove from the heat. Sift in the flour and ginger and beat well. Grease a baking sheet and put teaspoonfuls of the mixture on the baking sheet about 4 inches apart. Bake in the oven for 10 minutes until golden. Cool slightly, then carefully remove from the baking sheet and wrap round the handle of a wooden spoon. Leave for 2 minutes and then slip off the handle onto a wire rack and leave to cool. Fold the lemon juice and rind into the whipped cream. Place in a piping bag with a star nozzle and pipe a swirl of cream at each end of the brandy snaps.

FLAKY NUT TRIANGLES
Makes 16

4 oz (110 g) butter
2 oz (50 g) soft brown sugar
1 tsp ground cinnamon
8 oz (225 g) mixed nuts, chopped
14 oz (400 g) pkt frozen filo pastry, thawed
icing sugar for dusting

Preheat oven to 425°F/220°C/Gas Mk 7. Melt the butter. Use a little to grease an 11 x 7 inch (28 x 18 cm) rectangular tin. Mix together the sugar, cinnamon and nuts. Take two sheets of the pastry and use to line the tin. Brush with melted butter and sprinkle a quarter of the nut mixture over. Fold in the pastry edges. Repeat the layers until all the nut mixture is used up, buttering each layer of pastry and folding in the edges, finishing with a layer of pastry. Brush the final layer with butter and bake in a preheated oven for 15 minutes, then turn down the heat to 350°F/180°C/Gas Mk 4 for 10 minutes, until the pastry is golden. Sift icing sugar evenly over the top and return to the oven for another 5 minutes. Cut the pastry into 16 triangles with a very sharp knife. Serve warm dusted with a little extra icing sugar.

BETTY'S BROWNIES
Makes 16-20

6 oz (175 g) butter, melted
6 oz (175 g) caster sugar
1 tsp vanilla essence
1/4 tsp salt
3 eggs
2 oz (50 g) unsweetened cocoa powder
1/2 tsp baking powder
6 oz (175 g) plain flour
2 oz (50 g) chopped nuts

Preheat oven to 350°F/180°C/Gas Mk 4. Butter an 8 in (20 cm) square shallow cake tin. Combine the melted butter and sugar, beating well. Add the vanilla essence, salt and eggs and beat well again. Sift together the cocoa, baking powder and flour, and add to the mixture, mixing until smooth. Stir in the chopped nuts, pour into the tin and bake in the oven for 25-30 minutes until firm to the touch. Cool in the tin before cutting with a sharp knife. The brownies may be covered with chocolate icing before cutting.

DATE AND OAT CLUSTERS
Makes 20

4 oz (110 g) margarine
4 tbsp golden syrup
4 oz (110 g) plain chocolate
4 oz (110 g) chopped dates
6 oz (175 g) toasted oat cereal

Put the margarine and golden syrup in a small saucepan and slowly heat until the margarine has melted. Add the chocolate, broken into pieces, and stir until the chocolate has melted. Remove the pan from the heat and stir in the chopped dates and the oat cereal. Spoon into 20 paper cake cases and chill until set.

BUTTERFLY CAKES
Makes 18

4 oz (110 g) soft margarine
4 oz (110 g) caster sugar
2 eggs, size 3, separated
1 tbsp cold water
4 oz (110 g) wholemeal self-raising flour

Filling:
4 oz (110 g) soft margarine
4 oz (110 g) icing sugar
1 oz (25 g) walnuts, finely chopped

Preheat the oven to 350°F/180°C/Gas Mk 4. Cream the margarine and sugar together until light and fluffy. Beat in the two egg yolks and the cold water, and mix until well combined. Whisk the egg whites until they form soft peaks. Fold the flour into the creamed mixture, then gently fold in the whisked egg whites. Stand empty paper cake cases in a bun tin tray or on a baking sheet and place a heaped teaspoon of the mixture into each case. Bake in a preheated oven for 15-20 minutes until risen and golden. Cool on a wire rack. Cream together the margarine and icing sugar until light and fluffy. Stir in the finely chopped walnuts. When the cakes are cold, cut a small cone shape out of the top of each cake with a sharp knife. Put a heaped teaspoonful of the butter cream into each cavity. Cut each top in half and press the two halves into the butter cream to form butter-fly wings.

SPICY APPLE AND NUT BARS
Makes 18

3 oz (75 g) soft margarine
6 oz (175 g) caster sugar
2 eggs
3 oz (75 g) plain flour
1 tsp baking powder
1/2 tsp salt
1 tbsp unsweetened cocoa powder
1 tsp ground cinnamon
1/2 tsp grated nutmeg
1/4 tsp ground cloves
4 oz (110 g) oats
6 oz (175 g) diced peeled apple
2 oz (50 g) chopped mixed nuts
icing sugar

Preheat the oven to 375°F/190°C/Gas Mk 5. Lightly grease a 9 inch (23 cm) square baking tin. Cream the margarine and sugar until light and fluffy, and add the eggs one at a time, beating well in between each addition. Sift together the flour, baking powder, salt, cocoa powder and spices and fold into the egg mixture until just combined. Stir in the oats, apple and chopped nuts and turn into the prepared tin. Bake in a preheated oven for about 25 minutes or until the edges begin to shrink away from the sides of the tin. Cool completely before cutting and sprinkle with icing sugar.

FRUIT AND NUT REFRIGERATOR CAKE
Makes 8

5 oz (150 g) block of fruit and nut chocolate
4 oz (110 g) butter
2 tbsp golden syrup
5 oz (150 g) gingernut biscuits, crushed
2 oz (50 g) glacé cherries, quartered
8 whole blanched almonds

Break up the chocolate and melt in a basin over a pan of simmering water. Gently heat the butter and golden syrup together and stir in the crushed biscuits. Add the chocolate and glacé cherries. Pour into a 1 lb (450 g) loaf tin and arrange the almonds on top. Chill for at least 4 hours. Loosen the sides, ease out the cake and slice with a sharp knife.

LEMON CURD SHORTIES
Cuts into 8

4 oz (110 g) soft margarine
3 oz (75 g) caster sugar
1 egg, size 2
4 oz (110 g) plain flour
4 oz (110 g) self-raising flour
2 oz (50 g) softened butter
2 oz (50 g) caster sugar
1 egg, size 2
2 level tsp grated lemon rind
2 tbsp lemon juice

Preheat the oven to 350°F/180°C/Gas Mk 4. Cream the margarine and sugar together until light and fluffy, then beat in the egg. Sift the flours together and gradually work into the creamed mixture. Knead the dough into a ball, wrap in cling-film and chill in the refrigerator for about ½ hour. Put all the remaining ingredients into a bowl placed over a pan of gently simmering water. Stir until the sugar and butter have dissolved and the mixture is the consistency of thick cream. Leave to cool. Cut the dough in half and roll one half to fit a deep 7 inch (18 cm) flan tin. Line the tin, pressing the dough up the sides to make a shallow wall. Pour the cooled lemon curd over the shortcake base. Roll out the remaining dough to fit the tin and place over the lemon curd as a lid, pressing the edges firmly together. Place the tin on a baking sheet and bake in the top of the oven for 30-35 minutes. Leave to cool in the tin and sprinkle with caster sugar.

SHORTIE SWIRLS
Makes 15

4 oz (110 g) butter
1 oz (25 g) caster sugar
½ tsp vanilla essence
4 oz (110 g) plain flour

Preheat the oven to 350°F/180°C/Gas Mk 4. Beat the butter and sugar together until creamy. Beat in the vanilla essence, then gradually fold in the flour with a metal spoon. Spoon into a piping bag with a large rosette nozzle and pipe 15 swirls onto two lightly greased baking sheets. Bake in the centre of the oven for 20 minutes. Leave to cool on the trays, then remove and dust with icing sugar. These can be sandwiched together with a little jam and butter cream.

TWO CHOC REFRIGERATOR CAKE
Makes 12 fingers

6 oz (175 g) plain chocolate, broken into pieces
4 tbsp crunchy peanut butter
8 oz (225 g) gingernut biscuits, crushed
4 tbsp milk
4 oz (110 g) white chocolate
2 tbsp golden gyrup
1/2 oz (10 g) butter

Melt the plain chocolate in a small bowl placed over a pan of simmering water. As soon as it melts, remove from the heat and stir in the peanut butter. Stir the crushed biscuits into the chocolate mixture together with the milk. Spoon into a shallow 6 inch (15 cm) square cake tin. Break the white chocolate into pieces and place in a bowl with the golden syrup and butter. Place over a pan of hot water and stir until melted. Spread over the plain chocolate mixture and make a pattern on the top with the back of a fork. Chill in the refrigerator until set, then cut into fingers. Store in an airtight tin in a cool place.

GINGERBREAD MEN
Makes 12-15

4 oz (110 g) butter or soft margarine
4 level tbsp golden syrup
3 oz (75 g) dark brown sugar
8 oz (225 g) wholemeal self-raising flour
1 level tsp ground ginger
1 level tsp cinnamon
some currants to garnish

Preheat oven to 350°F/180°C/Gas Mk 4. Melt the butter or margarine, golden syrup and sugar in a small pan over gentle heat, stirring from time to time until the sugar melts. Do not let the mixture boil. Sift the flour and spices into a bowl, making a well in the centre. Pour in the syrup mixture, stirring from the centre outwards to incorporate all the flour. Turn out the mixture onto a lightly floured board and knead gently until it is smooth and binds together. Wrap in cling-film and refrigerate for 20 minutes. Roll out the mixture to about 1/8 inch (3 mm) thick and cut out gingerbread man shapes with cutters. Lay them on two greased baking sheets and make eyes and a mouth on each using the currants. Bake at the top of the oven for 15 minutes. Leave for 5 minutes before cooling on a wire tray.

GINGER ROLL

2 eggs, size 3
2 oz (50 g) caster sugar
2 oz (50 g) self-raising flour
1 tsp ground ginger
pinch ground mixed spice
1 oz (25 g) icing sugar
1 tbsp syrup from stem ginger
¼ pint (150 ml) double cream
2 oz (50 g) stem ginger

Preheat the oven to 400°F/200°C/Gas Mk 6. Line an 11 x 7 inch
(28 x 18 cm) Swiss roll tin with greased greaseproof paper. Put the
eggs and sugar together in a bowl over a saucepan of gently simmering water and whisk until the mixture is thick enough to leave a trail
when the whisk is lifted. Sift the flour with the spices and gently fold
in with a metal spoon. Turn into the prepared tin and level the surface. Bake in the oven for 10 minutes, or until the sponge springs back
when pressed. Place a sheet of greaseproof paper, 1 in (2.5 cm) larger
than the baking tin all round, on a board lightly sifted with icing
sugar. Turn out the sponge onto the icing sugar and peel off the lining
paper. Trim off the crisp edges and roll the sponge up gently, enclos-
ing the greaseproof paper. Leave to cool. Stir the ginger syrup into the
cream and whip until soft peaks form. Finely chop the stem ginger
and fold it into the cream. When the sponge is cool, unroll it, remove
the paper and fill the sponge with the ginger cream. Re-roll the filled
sponge. Sift with a little icing sugar and chill.

LEMON DIAMONDS
Makes 12

4 oz (110 g) soft margarine
4 oz (110 g) caster sugar
1 large egg, beaten
grated rind and juice of 1 lemon
4 oz (110 g) self-raising flour
1/2 tsp baking powder
3 oz (75 g) caster sugar

Preheat the oven to 350°F/180°C/Gas Mk 4. Cream the margarine and butter together until light and fluffy. Beat in the egg a little at a time together with the lemon rind, and finally sift in the mixed flour and baking powder. Turn the mixture into a greased 9 x 11 x 1 inch (23 x 28 x 2.5 cm) baking tin, generously dusted with flour, and bake in the centre of the oven for 20-25 minutes or until the sponge springs back when pressed with the fingertips. Warm the lemon juice in a small saucepan, stir in the sugar and heat gently until the sugar melts. Prick the cake all over with a fork and spoon over the lemon glaze. Leave to cool in the tin and then cut into diamonds.

MUNCHIE CRUNCHIES
Makes 8

1 oz (25 g) butter
1 level tbsp golden syrup
4 oz (110 g) plain chocolate, broken into pieces
1 level tbsp cocoa powder
3 oz (75 g) cornflakes
1/2 oz (10 g) preserved ginger or glacé cherries, chopped (optional)

Put the butter, golden syrup, chocolate and cocoa powder in a saucepan and heat gently until the butter and chocolate have melted. Carefully stir in the cornflakes and the fruit, if using. Mix gently until all is coated well with the chocolate and turn into a lightly greased 7½ x 7½ inch (19 x 19 cm) shallow tin. Press down lightly. Leave in the refrigerator to set and then cut into eight fingers

QUICK SPONGE SANDWICH
Serves 8

4 oz (110 g) soft margarine
4 oz (110 g) caster sugar
2 large eggs, beaten
4 oz (110 g) self-raising flour
1 level tsp baking powder
jam
double cream

Preheat the oven to 350°F/180°C/Gas Mk 4. Put all the ingredients in a large bowl and beat well for 2 minutes, preferably using an electric hand whisk or a mixer. Divide the mixture between two 7 inch (18 cm) sandwich tins, both greased and dusted with flour. Bake in the oven for 25-30 minutes until golden brown. Turn out onto a wire rack to cool. When they are cold, sandwich the two sponges together with plenty of jam of your choice. To make it rather special whip some double cream and add this on top of the jam. Sliced fresh or tinned fruit may also be added. Sprinkle the top with caster sugar.

INDEX

Anchovy toasts 22
Apple and cashew soup 6
Apple and date flapjacks 173
Apple scones 172
Apple slice 168
Apple snow 163
Apple tart 171
Apricot and oat crunchies 176
Apricot custard 158
Apricot fromage frais 156
Apricot refrigerator cake 178
Arabian meatballs 64
Arnold Bennett omelette 116

Bacon and egg scramble 43
Bacon and potato salad 143
Bacon fraize 43
Bacon risotto 123
Bacon rolls 49
Bacon rosti 41
Bacon stuffed trout 101
Bacon turnovers 45
Baconburgers 47
Baked Alaska 155
Baked apples 161
Baked eggs 109
Baked jam roll 161
Baked liver dumplings 71
Baked omelette 110
Baked salmon fillets 100
Basic minced beef 30
Basic minced lamb 56
Beef and bamboo shoots 34
Beef and cashew stir-fry 28
Beef and potato salad 143
Beef darioles 26
Betty's brownies 181
Boozy sausage casserole 46
Brandy snaps 180
Breast of chicken with walnut sauce 83
Broad beans with smoked bacon 48
Buck rarebit 26
Butterfly cakes 182

Cabbage parcels 38
Caramel walnut crunchies 179
Caribbean bananas 154
Caribbean chicken 78

Carrot and celery soup 8
Cauliflower cheese 137
Cheese and apple sandwiches 24
Cheese and mushroom bake 140
Cheese and mushroom noodles 132
Cheese and onion pudding 115
Cheese and onion soup 9
Cheese bake 107
Cheese custard 110
Cheese darioles 114
Cheese pancakes 115
Cheese sandwich pudding 112
Cheese stuffed potatoes 138
Cheese, anchovy and potato bake 91
Cheesy aubergines 138
Cheesy bacon slice 44
Cheesy baked loaf 111
Cheesy crumpets 108
Cheesy poached eggs 106
Cheesy pudding 110
Cheesy soufflé potatoes 136
Cheesy stuffed mushrooms 141
Cheesy tomato bake 139
Cheesy topped gammon 42
Chicken and mango salad 144
Chicken and mushroom sandwiches 17
Chicken and sweetcorn 79
Chicken and sweetcorn chowder 7
Chicken and tomato scramble 18
Chicken breasts in port 77
Chicken breasts with cinnamon 75
Chicken cacciatore 79
Chicken cocottes 78
Chicken jerez 80
Chicken Julienne 76
Chicken liver bagels 14
Chicken liver mash 65
Chicken livers on toast 15
Chicken pilaff 124
Chicken ragout with cardamom 84
Chicken tetrazzini 127
Chicken Waldorf salad 149
Chicken with bacon and capers 83
Chick pea and leek salad 151
Chilli beef stir-fry 29
Chilli con carne 30
Chinese beef stir-fry 37
Chinese drumsticks 18

Choc and nut squares *178*
Chocolate and banana whip *165*
Chocolate nut sundae *154*
Cider bacon chops *41*
Cinnamon drop scones *177*
Cinnamon shortbreads *173*
Coconut fingers *176*
Coconut macaroons *172*
Cod parcels *96*
Corn savoury *140*
Corned beef and sweetcorn double-decker *16*
Country fish bake *100*
Crab mayonnaise *92*
Crab toasts *21*
Cream of spinach soup *11*
Cream of watercress soup *10*
Creamed ham on toast *16*
Crispy macaroni beef *33*
Croque monsieur *12*
Cubana egg rice *120*
Curd tart *177*
Curried cheese rice *118*
Curried mince with apricots *28*
Curried parsnip soup *10*

Date and oat clusters *182*
Devilled cheese *23*
Devilled chicken *77*
Devilled fillet of sole *99*
Dutch pepper soup *11*

Eastern chicken salad *145*
Egg and bacon au gratin *48*
Egg and bacon pots *117*
Egg and chive sandwiches *23*
Egg and ham Florentine *47*
Egg ratatouille *114*
Eggs baked in sausage *107*
Eggs en cocotte *107*
Eggs Florentine *117*
Eggs in nests *105*
Eggs in onion sauce *116*
Eggs with spinach *112*
Eggs with tuna mayonnaise *108*
Egg, liver and mushroom bake *70*
Ely chops *58*

Farmhouse eggs *113*
Festive pears *169*
Fillet of lamb with redcurrant sauce *60*
Fish and egg bake *101*
Fish cakes *102*

Fish casserole *97*
Fish charlotte *97*
Fish meunière *95*
Fisherman's pie *89*
Flaky nut triangles *181*
Florentines *180*
Fluffy eggs *106*
French onion soup *9*
Fresh fruit salad *158*
Fruit and nut refrigerator cake *183*
Fruit crumble *162*
Fruit fool *153*

Gala pears *156*
German pork chops *45*
Giant spicy beefburgers *29*
Ginger pears *170*
Ginger roll *186*
Gingerbread men *185*
Gingered Japanese chicken *82*
Glazed gammon steaks *44*
Glazed mint chops *57*
Grilled sardines *88*

Haddock and courgette bake *94*
Ham and chicken double-decker *17*
Ham and cream cheese triple-decker *14*
Ham and noodles *126*
Ham scramble *53*
Ham wrapped chicken *82*
Herring and apple salad *150*
Honey lamb chops *54*
Hot bean rarebit *142*
Hot chicken and rocket salad *146*
Hungarian pork fillets *46*

Indian pittas *19*
Indian scramble *25*
Irish kidneys *65*
Italian cauliflower salad *152*
Italian style meatballs *32*

Kedgeree *91*
Kidney and onion soup *6*
Kidney bean rarebit *22*
Kidney toasts *73*
Kidneys à l'orange *67*
Kidneys and batter *66*
Kidneys jerez *69*
Kippered eggs *108*

Lamb and apricot sauté *59*
Lamb chop and plum grill *57*

Lamb chops with ratatouille *62*
Lamb Florentine *61*
Lamb in lemon and garlic *63*
Lamb paprika-style *59*
Lamb salad with almonds *145*
Leek and bacon risotto *119*
Leeks in cheese sauce *139*
Lemon cheese fluff *159*
Lemon curd shorties *184*
Lemon diamonds *187*
Lemon puffs *170*
Linguine with tomatoes and basil *130*
Liver and beans *69*
Liver and onions *70*
Liver and satsumas *73*
Liver in Cointreau *72*
Liver Italiano *74*
Liver ragout *67*
Liver risotto *119*
Liver with sage and Madeira sauce *68*

Macaroni cheese *130*
Macaroni with frankfurters *135*
Malayan fish *98*
Mandarin cream *160*
Mango magic *159*
Marbled mallow cakes *179*
Marmalade sandwich pudding *164*
Marzipan apples *165*
Mediterranean bean stew *142*
Melon and tongue salad *146*
Mexican egg bake *103*
Mexican steak *36*
Mince hot pot *34*
Mint lamb burgers and cucumber *61*
Muffin pizzas *15*
Munchie crunchies *187*
Mushroom and sherry soup *8*
Mushroom and tuna bake *93*
Mushroom muffins *21*
Mushroom pilaff *123*
Mustard and apple lamb chops *55*
Mustard chicken *81*

Neptune risotto *118*
Neptune's burgers *92*
Normandy casserole *51*
Normandy chicken *75*
Normandy cod *99*

Oaty cheese burgers *105*
Olive and cabbage salad *151*
Orange and cranberry mince *33*

Orange meatballs *31*
Orange pots *160*
Oriental kidneys *71*
Oriental pork and prawns *50*
Oxford sausages *40*
Oxford steaks with caper sauce *58*

Paella *122*
Pancakes *166*
Pasta bows with mushrooms and bacon *133*
Pasta with ham and cheese *134*
Peach and raspberry streusel *174*
Peach melba *155*
Peach surprise *168*
Pear and ginger fromage frais *154*
Penne Tuscany *126*
Pesto pasta *128*
Picnic tart *52*
Pineapple cream *167*
Piperade *104*
Piquant bacon chops *51*
Piquant kidneys *66*
Pitta pockets *24*
Poached halibut *98*
Pork chops with cheese and beer *39*
Pork fillet with mustard cream sauce *40*
Pork with plum sauce *39*
Portmanteau lamb chops *62*
Portuguese kidneys *68*
Potato and egg fritters *137*
Poultry loaves *76*

Quick cheesecakes *163*
Quick chocolate cake *175*
Quick haddock kedgeree *120*
Quick sponge sandwich *188*

Raspberry melon delight *156*
Ratafia strawberries *157*
Red Leicester and salad double-decker *25*
Regency rice *122*
Rhubarb and ginger *164*
Risotto à la fromage *121*
Roast pork salad *147*
Rolled plaice *94*
Rosy kissel *167*

Salad Niçoise *148*
Salmon steaks with vegetables *95*
Sandwich kebabs *13*
Saucy spicy eggs *117*
Sausage and rice salad *148*

Sauté chicken 80
Savoury fritters 19
Savoury liver with noodles 131
Scallops au gratin 93
Scotch woodcock 20
Scottish stovies 36
Seafood risotto 121
Shepherd's pie 60
Shortie swirls 184
Sirloin steaks with mustard 32
Smoked chicken and cheese toasts 13
Smoked haddock cocottes 89
Smoked mackerel and egg
double-decker 20
Soft roe fingers 24
Somerset cider gammon 49
Soufflé omelette 104
Spaghetti Milanese 134
Spaghetti western 127
Spaghetti with smoked haddock 129
Spanish chicken 81
Spanish churros 175
Spanish eggs 113
Spanish ham salad 144
Spanish lamb 54
Spanish omelette 111
Spanish rice 125
Spicy apple and nut bars 183
Spicy cod kebabs 90
Spicy ham and cheese toasts 16
Spicy prawn noodles 129
Spicy rhubarb sponge 166
Spinach pots 136
Spring lamb with vegetables 63
Steak and onions 27
Steak chasseur 37
Steak Diane 35
Stilton steaks 31
Strawberries Romanoff 157
Strawberry syllabub 161
Sweet and sour meatballs 38
Swiss bacon chop 42

Tagliatelle and mushrooms 125
Tagliatelle verdi with salmon 128
Tagliolini and fresh herb sauce 131
Tandoori bacon chops with rice 50
Tangy lamb chops 56
Tetrazzini ramekins 133
Three egg omelette 109
Tomato and egg savoury 103
Tomato surprise 102
Treacle tart 162

Tropical rock cakes 174
Trout and almonds 90
Tuna and cheese with dill 88
Tuna and macaroni layer pie 132
Tuna and rice salad 149
Turkey and broccoli 86
Turkey and yoghurt salad 150
Turkey breasts in Marsala 85
Turkey cream salad 147
Turkey escalopes with hazelnuts 84
Turkey Italienne 87
Turkey risotto 124
Turkey savoury 85
Turkey stroganoff 86
Turkish mince 35
Turkish oranges 169
Tuscan casserole 53
Two choc refrigerator cake 185

Vegetable soup 12

Welsh liver 72
Welsh pork chops 52
Welsh rarebit 23
White fish chowder 7

Yorkshire lamb cutlets 55

Zabaglione 153
Zeus steaks 27